Aug 2004

Jim Scott
972/473-8636
5713 GLENEAGLES DR
PLANO, TX 75093

D0115492

He Knows My Name: A Forty Day Encounter With Christ
Paul W. Arndt - 1st ed.
p. cm.
ISBN 0-9727903-1-4 (alk. paper)
FLC Works® Publishing

Scripture taken from *THE MESSAGE*:
Copyright ©1993, 1994, 1995, 1996, 2000, 2001 & 2002.
Used by permission of NavPress Publishing Group.
All rights reserved.

THE MESSAGE is trademarked and is
registered in the United States Patent and Trademark Office by
International Bible Society.

Written, Designed, Printed and Manufactured proudly
in the United States of America

FIRST PRINTING

To My Wife and Two Sons

Faye Marie

More than anyone else you help me believe that ...

Christ is for me
Christ lives in me
Christ works through me
And that Christ is with me.

Joshua and Jacob

Thanks for reminding me that the
"lost children's area" is for lost dads too.

Acknowledgements

To the Ministry Leadership Team, Discipleship Team, and Staff at Faith Lutheran Church

Christ's heart beats fast in your life. My prayer is
that the vision the Savior has given you for this book
will pulse through all who read it.

To My Family and All of Those Who Prayed While I Wrote this Book

More times than *you* could ever know, I
was ready to drop the pen, walk away from my desk,
and quit. More times than *I* will ever know, you
dropped to your knees and asked the Good Shepherd
to carry me to the finish.

To Daniel Nagy

Book projects are like passing guests, they
come and then they go but friendships stay and make
themselves at home. Thanks for the long hours made
short by heartfelt conversation.

To Mike Imirie

It's one thing to write about Christ; it's another to
write about him clearly. You've helped me do both.
Thanks for your keen eye and your kind words.

READ BEFORE FIRST SMALL GROUP SESSION

Contents

Shelter of Provision

"GOD, my shepherd! I don't need a thing."
(Psalm 23:1)

Shelter of Peace

*"You have bedded me down in lush meadows, you
find me quiet pools to drink from."*
(Psalm 23:2)

Shelter of Rest

"True to your word, you let me catch my breath,
and send me in the right direction."
(Psalm 23:3)

Shelter of Safety

"Even when the way goes through Death Valley, I'm not
afraid when you walk at my side. Your trusty shepherd's
crook makes me feel secure."
(Psalm 23:4)

Shelter of Celebration

"You serve me a six-course dinner right in front of my enemies.
You revive my drooping head; my cup brims with blessing."
(Psalm 23:5)

Shelter of Love

"Your beauty and love chase after me every day of my life."
(Psalm 23:6a)

Shelter of Eternal Dwelling

"I'm back home in the house of GOD for the rest of my life."
(Psalm 23:6b)

Prologue

"He calls his own sheep by name ..."

John 10:3

Paul. That's my name.

I answer to it. I listen for it. When someone shouts it in a crowd, my ears perk; my head turns; and my eyes scan for a familiar face. When you speak my name, you get my attention.

I have other names. Some are formal: "Reverend", "Pastor", "Mr. Paul Warren Arndt." Others are descriptive: "Spiritual Counselor", "Leader", "Writer." Still others are more intimate: "Husband", "Father", "Son", and "Friend." The name you use marks the type of relationship you have with me. Knowing my name is the first step in knowing me.

But there's more to me than my name. "Paul" is just the gateway to the rest of who I am. Speak it and you just might open a door to another world—a world far more complex than a one-syllable word of identification.

Beneath my name are disappointments and dreams, failure and redemption, loss and triumph, worry and gratitude, fear and faith, panic and peace, pride and humility, sorrow and joy, death and life, sinner and saint. These particulars are more than my name; they're my life. If you dare to break the surface waters of my name and dive into the depths of my life, then you'll really know me. But it all begins with my name.

The good news is that, before your parents spoke your name, it was already rolling off the tip of the Good Shepherd's tongue. Jesus, the Christ, knows your name.

He whispers it in your ear when you feel alone. When you're lost and can't find your way, he shouts it above, in, and over the noise of your world. He weeps over it when you go astray. As he searches for you, he climbs the highest summit and scans the horizon, all the while crying out your name. From the cross he shouts it until the saving echo of his voice reaches your ears.

As you journey through this book, I want you to hear the Good Shepherd speak your name. I want you to encounter Christ. My prayer is that he'll meet you in every sentence that you read, surprise you in every word that you write, find you in every prayer that you pray, and come upon you with every thought that you think. When you finish, I hope that you will have come to realize that he knows more than your name.

He knows you.

Each day in this forty-day encounter with Christ begins with a selected portion from one of the Gospels. Before you begin the meditation, read the text from your own Bible.

As you read, ask the following questions,

> In what way does Christ know my name?
> How does he know me?

Following each reading is a brief meditation centered on the Scripture. Read the meditation with a receptive heart. As you read, ask Christ to meet you. The words aren't perfect; neither are the thoughts behind them. Together, though, they may be a means by which Christ chooses to speak.

Throughout the body of the meditations, I've chosen to use Eugene Petersen's paraphrase of the Bible called *THE MESSAGE*. Its tone, voice, and language are easy on the eye, pleasant to the ear, and soothing to the heart. It also has a narrative quality that adds a beautiful harmony line to the melody of the meditations.

After the meditation is a section for reflection. As with anything that requires work, the reward received is in direct proportion to the effort you invest. What you get out of this section is a direct result of what you're willing to put in.

As you reflect on the questions, it might be helpful to keep a separate spiritual journal—a safe place to record sacred and intimate thoughts. Throw yourselves into the questions. Think deeply about them. Take the time and expend the energy necessary to ponder the work and words of Christ in your life.

Finally, there is a prayer. Use the prayer to focus, direct, and capture the desire of your heart. Apply it to your situation in life. Come back to the prayer throughout the day and allow it to do whatever work Christ may choose.

Scattered throughout the meditations are seven "shelters"—still moments, places of retreat, days to sit, rest, and catch your breath during the forty-day encounter.

Each "shelter" is built on the foundation of the Twenty-Third Psalm.

The first is a shelter of provision:
"God, my shepherd! I don't need a thing."

The second is a place of peace:
"lush meadows and quiet pools to drink from."

The third gives a new beginning:
"you let me catch my breath and send me in the right direction."

The fourth provides safety:
"a trusty shepherd's crook."

The fifth is a moment of celebration:
"a six-course dinner and a cup that brims with blessing."

The sixth lavishes goodness and love:
"beauty and love chase after me every day of my life."

Finally, the seventh promises an eternal dwelling:
"back home in the house of God for the rest of my life." [1]

> Forty encounters.
> Seven shelters.
> One Savior—a Shepherd
> who knows your name.

In the words and pages that follow, the Good Shepherd wants to go beyond formal introductions. He's not satisfied with superficial pleasantries. No more cordial chitchat. He wants to burrow his way to the innermost place—he in you and you in him.

> He wants to know you and you to know him.
> He wants to love you and you to love him.
> He wants to serve you and you to serve him.

That's an encounter with Christ. And it all begins with your name.

paul

---

[1] Psalm 23

Before You Begin

When it comes to the words and ways of God, our human reason quarrels with Christ's divine revelation. We demand logical answers to questions loaded with mystery.

In our attempt to know God, we strive to climb the ladder of reason and peer into the hidden things of heaven. We want to understand those things that are higher and deeper and wider than we are—the way God works and what he thinks. But the ladder of reason is short and it stands many rungs shy of heaven's secrets.

Christ is mystery—the Word in existence before time.

Christ is revelation—the Word made flesh in time.

Christ is encounter—today, right now, the Word living and active, approaching and reproaching, always surprising, mystifying.

As the Apostle Paul wrote in his letter to the Colossians,

> *The mystery in a nutshell is just this: Christ is in you, therefore you can look forward to sharing in God's glory. It's that simple. That is the substance of our Message.* [1]

Christ in us. There is no greater intimacy. It's that simple and that profound.

In your life, when explanations won't do, logic won't satisfy, and reason fails to bring any comfort, Christ promises to encounter you. He wants to meet you where you are, as you are. That's the life-changing experience that awaits us in every moment of every day.

Before you begin your journey, write a prayer in your journal describing your desire for these forty days.

[1]Colossians 1:27

Day 1:
He Knows My Family Tree

Scripture Reading: Matthew 1:1, 16-17

Meditation

When the Father sent his Son into the world, he placed him in the care of a frail, human family. Though he was the only begotten fruit of the Father, Jesus fell from the limb of Abraham and David's family tree.

At his birth, the Son of God was given a set of fingerprints, a birth certificate, and a first and last name. God became Jesus, the Christ, the *son* of David, the *son* of Abraham. The Alpha and the Omega—the one who had no beginning and no end—suddenly had ancestors, a lineage, and a genealogy. Eternity became a part of recorded history.

The Son of God was no distant deity. In the incarnation, the great I AM became a child of the patriarchs; the Prince of Peace dove into the gene pool of kings; and the Messiah transfused himself into the bloodline of humanity.

He became the son of Abraham—the child of promise.

All nations on Earth will find themselves blessed through your descendants because you obeyed me. [1]

He became the son of David—the promised heir of a king

A green Shoot [Jesus] *will sprout from Jesse's stump, from his roots a budding Branch.* [2]

1

He became the firstborn son of a working class family—the son of a carpenter named Joseph, the husband of Mary.

> *Jacob had Joseph, Mary's husband,*
> *the Mary who gave birth to Jesus,*
> *the Jesus who was called Christ.* [3]

Though the Promised Seed of the woman would bear much fruit, the family tree from which Jesus came had more than its share of knots, splinters, and broken limbs.

> Its patriarchal roots ran shallow.
> Its Messianic trunk was twisted.·
> It's kingly limbs bore rotten fruit.

When God told an arthritic Abraham and a sterile Sarah that they would soon be moving from the geriatric ward to the maternity ward, the two senior citizens looked at each other, shook their heads, and laughed at the promise. The promise was planted but faith had yet to take root.

> *God continued speaking to Abraham, "And Sarai your wife: Don't call her Sarai any longer; call her Sarah. I'll bless her—yes! I'll give you a son by her! Oh, how I'll bless her! Nations will come from her; kings of nations will come from her."*
>
> *Abraham fell flat on his face. And then he laughed, thinking, "Can a hundred-year-old man father a son? And can Sarah, at ninety years, have a baby?"* [4]

Sexual abomination, indiscretions, and mixed marriages twisted the trunk of the Messianic tree. Incest between Judah and his daughter-in-law, Tamar, produced twin boys, Perez and Zerah. Rahab, the great grandmother of King David, was the prostitute who had hidden the spies when they came to Jericho. Ruth, the grandmother of King David, was a Gentile, a foreigner, and an outsider but she married Boaz and was grafted into the Messianic tree.

> *Salmon had Boaz (his mother was Rahab),*
> *Boaz had Obed (Ruth was the mother),*
> *Obed had Jesse,*
> *Jesse had David,*
>   *and David became king.* 5

The kingly limbs were no better. The ground below their royal branches reeked of rotten fruit. King David was said to be a man after God's own heart, yet his heart beat fast for Uriah's wife. When he saw Bathsheba bathing, lust conceived a plot and deception brought it full term. Adultery gave birth to murder.

> *David had Solomon (Uriah's wife was the mother).* 6

Though the branches of the messianic tree tried to twist the purpose of the Father, the love of the Messiah never turned. His lineage was a genealogy of grace. Hanging from another tree, he would declare that no family was beyond redemption, no sin past the point of forgiveness, and no sinner too far from the extended arms of God. He answered to the name of Jesus—"God saves."

> *She (Mary) will bring a son to birth, and when she does,*
> *you, Joseph, will name him Jesus—"God saves"—because*
> *he will save his people from their sins. This would bring*
> *the prophet's embryonic sermon to full term:*
>
> *Watch for this—a virgin will get pregnant and bear a*
> *son; they will name him Emmanuel (Hebrew for "God is*
> *with us").* 7

In Jesus, God has come near.

Divinity is no longer distant, nor detached. He is Emmanuel—"God is with us." Heaven's Seed has planted himself in the soil of earth. Messiah has rooted himself deep into his creation. Grace, mercy, and peace have grafted themselves into the family tree of humanity and the fruit of that tree is forgiveness—the taste of sweet salvation.

Reflection

In what ways has Jesus worked in your family in spite of its past? How has he redeemed the knots, splinters, and rotten fruit of your family tree?

How is your lineage a genealogy of grace?

How have you been grafted into the tree of salvation?

What does it mean to be rooted in Christ Jesus?

Prayer

Father,

Your Son was the promised Seed of salvation. Though the fruit of your heaven was perfect, the family tree from which he fell was not. His ancestors had more than their share of knots, splinters, twisted branches, broken limbs, and rotten fruit. But when good genes went bad, your grace covered the ages. In generation after generation after generation, you redeemed rebellion, sanctified the stain of sin, and protected the promise of Messiah.

During this day, help me remember that I am a descendant of Jesus the Christ, the son of David, the son of Abraham. Though my family tree may be gnarled, crooked, and twisted, assure me that my life is rooted in the cross of Christ. Give me faith to believe that I am grafted into the tree of salvation. Though my past is imperfect, remind me that Jesus the Christ can still use me. It's in the name of the son of Abraham that I pray.

Amen.

[1]Genesis 22:18 [2]Isaiah 11:1 [3]Matthew 1:16 [4]Genesis 17:15-17
[5]Matthew 1:5-6 [6]Matthew 1:6 [7]Matthew 1:21-23

Day 2:
He Knows My Questions
Scripture Reading: Luke 1:26-38

Meditation

Up until today, the only questions that have kept Mary's mind racing are the ones that have to do with her upcoming wedding to Joseph.

"Who should we invite? How many?
Where should we have the banquet?
What should I wear?"

But when Gabriel, the archangel of heaven, arrives with a pair of blue baby booties, Mary's well-planned world shakes like the rattle her son will soon hold.

"Good morning!
You're beautiful with God's beauty,
Beautiful inside and out!
God be with you."

She was thoroughly shaken, wondering what was behind a greeting like that. But the angel assured her, "Mary, you have nothing to fear. God has a surprise for you: You will become pregnant and give birth to a son and call his name Jesus. [1]

For a young girl about to be married, a child out of wedlock is scandalous. In an instant, Mary's life changes. Her thoughts go from being a bride to becoming a single mother, from a honeymoon to the maternity ward, and from dancing with her new husband under the stars to changing diapers late into the night. Out go the wedding plans; in come the questions.

"What's God up to? Why me? Why of all times, now?
How can this be? I'm not married yet."

Mary's questions try to squeeze the faith out of her life. Though the announcement came via an angel, Mary wonders if God really knows what he's doing. After all, a virgin can't conceive. And one about to get married—she better not conceive! It would be a violation of the pledge that she swore to Joseph and grounds for divorce. Potentially it's a death sentence. Gabriel must have come to the wrong house. He must have the wrong girl because it's definitely the wrong time.

For Mary, a baby is a dream yet to be dreamt. It's a desire planted and due to sprout sometime in the future, after the wedding. But first things need to be first: marriage, husband, stability, and then a child. Gabriel's announcement is unreasonable. Unthinkable. Impossible.

Confused, Mary asks the archangel for an explanation.

"But how? I've never slept with a man." [2]

Gabriel answers,

"The Holy Spirit will come upon you,
the power of the Highest hover over you;
Therefore, the child you bring to birth
will be called Holy, Son of God." [3]

His explanation is a mystery. Somehow, some way, heaven's Son is going to take on human flesh. The Holy Spirit will plant the Promised Seed in Mary and Salvation will take root. The Seed of Heaven will grow, mature, and kick strong within his mother's womb. Messiah's majesty will be veiled for nine months but, when he is born, he will be called Holy, the Son of God.

Though this work of the Father will radically alter Mary's life, he doesn't give her all of the answers. He simply assures her that, in the middle of the mystery, he is working. He doesn't explain the fullness of what he's doing, or how, or why. He chooses to keep many of the divine details to himself and leaves Mary's questions unanswered.

Though Mary's perplexed, Gabriel reminds her that, in the mystery of it all, God is with her. The power of the Almighty overshadows her. He has a surprise for her—the Christ child will not only grow in her womb, one day she'll cradle him in her arms.

Noticing that Mary is still puzzled by the Father's surprise, Gabriel presents Mary with a parting gift. Along with the birth announcement, he delivers a full resume of her unborn son's future accomplishments. It's enough to make any mother beam.

> *"He will be great,*
> *be called 'Son of the Highest.'*
> *The Lord God will give him*
> *the throne of his father David;*
> *He will rule Jacob's house forever—*
> *no end, ever, to his kingdom."* [4]

In the midst of the mystery, God takes Mary's questions, gently straightens them out, stands them up, brushes them off, and turns them into an exclamation of surrender. Though fearful, she relinquishes control.

Mary lets the questions remain questions, abandons the demand for answers, and gives herself over to the loving hands of the Father.

> *"Yes, I see it all now:*
> *I'm the Lord's maid, ready to serve.*
> *Let it be with me*
> *just as you say."* [5]

Reflection

What questions do you have for the Father?

Have you ever been thoroughly shaken by an action or announcement of God?

In what ways have you asked God, *"How can this be?"*

How is God straightening out your questions and turning them into an exclamation of surrender—*"let it be with me just as you say"*?

Prayer

Father,

When you work in my life, I have questions. I don't always understand what you're doing, how you're doing it, or why. Your ways are higher than my ways and what you think goes beyond what I can imagine. When I ask for answers, you don't always give me the details but you do assure me that your Son is always with me and with him all things are possible.

During this day, when your heavenly messengers come with a divine proclamation, I want to listen. Though I shake, don't let me be afraid. Though I question, help me believe. Though I wonder, help me submit. Like Mary, help me embrace your good news even though it seems to come at the wrong time. Through your Son, gently straighten out my questions, stand them up, and turn them into exclamations of praise—points of surrender. Each day, every moment, let it be with me as you say. It's in your Son's name that I pray.

Amen.

[1]Luke 1:28-31 [2]Luke 1:34 [3]Luke 1:35 [4]Luke 1:32-33 [5]Luke 1:38

Day 3:
He Knows My Emotions

Scripture Reading: Luke 1:39-80

Meditation

Expectant mothers, more than others, are filled with emotion.

As they sit next to the empty-but-ready cradles, they dream God-sized dreams for their unborn children. They glow with anticipation. As the due date draws close, each mother-in-waiting rocks anxiously. But when the baby is born, joy rushes in. The promise is fulfilled. The dream-come-true lays its head, fast asleep, in its mother's arms. The waiting is over. The time has finally come and the baby brings with it a song.

Mary's a virgin yet she is about to become a first time mother. She's expecting a child but she doesn't know what to expect. Still startled and confused by all that the angel had said, she needs to talk to someone who might understand. The only one who might be able to believe the impossible annunciation from Gabriel is another in whom the impossible has been conceived—her cousin Elizabeth, the one who was once barren and said to be beyond years.

Mary is in her first trimester; her cousin, Elizabeth, is in her third. Both have divine expectations about the child within their wombs. One child is promised to be a prophet, the other the Messiah. As each child grows, so do the emotions. Joy mixes with anxiety. Happiness mingles with fear. And laughter continues to trade places with panic.

After Gabriel's message, Mary immediately packs her bags. She scribbles a note for Joseph telling him where she's going but she doesn't tell him when she'll be back. She doesn't know if she'll be back. When you're an unwed, pregnant virgin said to be carrying the Son of God, who knows what the future holds? With worries as heavy as her bags, she begins the fifty-mile trip from Nazareth to Elizabeth's home in Judea.

As soon as Mary enters Elizabeth's house, the rhythm of a salvation song begins. John the Baptist, sixth months in his mother's womb, is the first one to hear Mary's voice. With a kick of recognition, he starts and keeps a steady beat up against the sides of his mother's womb.

> *When Elizabeth heard Mary's greeting, the baby in her womb leaped. She was filled with the Holy Spirit, and sang out exuberantly ...*[1]

All Mary has the chance to do is shout a greeting. Before she can say a word about anything that has happened, Elizabeth, filled by the Holy Spirit and prompted by the driving beat set by her son, begins to sing,

> *"You're so blessed among women,*
> *   and the babe in your womb, also blessed!*
> *And why am I so blessed that*
> *   the mother of my Lord visits me?*
> *Blessed woman, who believed what God said,*
> *   believed every word would come true!"* [2]

The song is Spirit-strong. It calms Mary's soul and soothes her spirit. Being further along in her pregnancy, Elizabeth seems to understand the plan that God has conceived. Her son, John, will be born first. He'll be the forerunner, preparing the way for Mary's son, Jesus. Together, their births will bring a redemptive song. Jesus will sing the melody and John the backup harmony.

Elizabeth's song unearths the treasure that Mary has buried deep in her heart: this pregnancy isn't a curse; it's a blessing. In the months to come there may be many cultural consequences: an angry and accusing fiancé; the disgrace of divorce; whispers of gossip from the women gathered around the well; the shame and struggle of being a single parent.

This pregnancy may bring all sorts of burdens but—come what may—this child isn't a burden to bear; it's a blessing to embrace. What's more, through this pregnancy, Mary will be blessed, blessed among all women.

Comforted by Elizabeth's song, Mary begins her own.

"I'm bursting with God-news; I'm dancing the song of
my Savior God.
God took one good look at me, and look what
happened—I'm the most fortunate woman on earth!
What God has done for me will never be forgotten,
the God whose very name is holy, set apart from
all others." 3

When John is born three months later, Zechariah, his father, adds another stanza.

"Blessed be the Lord, the God of Israel;
he came and set his people free.
He set the power of salvation in the center of our
lives, and in the very house of David his servant..." 4

Throughout the centuries, Messianic expectations flooded the human soul with emotions. When the promise of Messiah was given to the Patriarchs, joy leaped. When its fulfillment was delayed, each generation grit its teeth and shook an angry fist heavenward. In the Exile, when the Promised Seed appeared to be all but lost, sorrow grabbed hold of the gut and doubled it over in grief.

Joy. Anger. Sorrow. These are the emotions of those who wait for the Messiah. But when the Messiah finally comes, joy belts out a song.

His birth fulfills all expectations and floods the emotions. And all those around him can't help but sing a salvation song.

Reflection

1) What emotions mix and mingle with your faith?

   When joy comes, what salvation songs do you sing?

   Write your own song of praise.

   Begin stanza one with, *"I'm bursting with God-news ..."*

   Begin stanza two with, *"Blessed be ..."*

1) Unworthy
   weakness + doubt

Prayer

Father,

Like the ancients of old, my emotions are tied to expectations. When good news comes, joy leaps and sings a song. When my dreams are frustrated, anger shakes a fist heavenward. When there is loss, sorrow grabs hold of my gut and grief stabs at my heart. These emotions are powerful. They're external representations of my inner faith—a mirror of the depths of my heart. They're spontaneous, authentic, reflexive reactions of my spirit.

During this day, when loss brings me sorrow, may the Christ child that lives in me give me hope. When pain brings me frustration, anger, or rage, may he grant me peace. Like Elizabeth, when the pleasure of a fulfilled promise brings me joy, may he gift me with a song. As I worship with all of my emotions, help me sing like Mary,

"I'm bursting with God-news ...".

And when I pray, add the harmony of Zechariah's song,

"Blessed be ...".

Like the mother of God, may all that I do, all that I say, and all that I feel reflect the Christ child that lives in me. It's in his name that I pray.

Amen.

[1]Luke 1:41-42 [2]Luke 1:41-42,45 [3]Luke 1;46-49 [4]Luke 1:68-69

Day 4:
He Knows My Dreams
Scripture Reading: Matthew 1:18-25

Meditation

Joseph's a practical man with practical plans.

He's a carpenter. His life, like his work, is deliberate. He always starts with a set of blueprints. First he plans his work and then he works his plan. He measures twice so that he only has to cut once. He lives by the absolute of the plumb line. He makes sure everything fits, and then, when it's all in place, he nails it down, snug and square. For Joseph, everything has to be on the level.

He's a simple man with simple dreams: a wife, a family, and a new home at the edge of the village—one that he's building for his bride-to-be, Mary. But his fiancée is about to shatter the foundation of his dreams.

> *The birth of Jesus took place like this. His mother, Mary, was engaged to be married to Joseph. Before they came to the marriage bed, Joseph discovered she was pregnant. (It was by the Holy Spirit, but he didn't know that.)* [1]

"Joseph, I'm pregnant." These three words turn Joseph's dreams into a nightmare.

Mary's words rip out the cornerstone, destroy the footings, and tear down the finished walls of Joseph's practical plans. Before Joseph can catch his breath, his dreams collapse. Hope lays twisted on the ground and disappointment takes up residence in the rubble.

Though Mary tries to explain that the Holy Spirit is the one who conceived her child, her words are perceived as betrayal. Months earlier, she had made a vow of fidelity to Joseph. She had publicly pledged her purity and chastity. Her engagement was a legal and binding promise that could only be broken by a writ of divorce. Infidelity of any kind, in any way, at any stage in the relational contract was tantamount to adultery and good reason for stoning.

Though distraught by the news, Joseph tries to remain a righteous man. He wants to do the right thing, both by Mary and before God. He not only wants to do the right thing, he wants to do the right thing the right way. He wants to live both by love and by the letter of the Law. Trying to reconcile how he can do both, he seeks the will of God. He searches his heart, in spite of the hurt.

The letter of the Law persuades him to divorce Mary but love pushes him to divorce Mary but love pushes him to do it in such a way as to protect her..

Joseph, chagrined but noble, determined to take care of things quietly so Mary would not be disgraced. [2]

Divorce.

Though the decision is difficult, it comes from a clean heart. It has been washed with many tears, purified through hours of prayer, and sanctified through godly counsel. It's the best answer Joseph has for a devastating situation saturated with painful, unanswered questions.

"Mary, who's the father? Why'd you do it?
"Didn't I make you happy?"

So as not to disgrace Mary, Joseph chooses to divorce her quietly. He would sign the necessary legal papers privately so that Mary wouldn't be judged in public.

His mind is set and so is his heart. But then an angel appears.

> *"Joseph, son of David, don't hesitate to get married. Mary's pregnancy is Spirit-conceived. God's Holy Spirit has made her pregnant. She will bring a son to birth, and when she does, you, Joseph, will name him Jesus— 'God saves'—because he will save his people from their sins."* [3]

"Don't hesitate." With two words from the angel, Joseph's nightmare turns back into a dream. The angel confirms what Mary had been trying to explain all along.

There was no betrayal.
No infidelity. No deceit.

The son conceived in her is from the seed of the Holy Spirit. Though pregnant, she is still a virgin.

When God chooses to give birth to his Dream, the well-planned and well-prayed dreams of Mary and Joseph shatter. But when one dream dies, God gives birth to another.

Into the disappointment that comes with the miscarriage of Mary and Joseph's well-conceived dreams, the Father implants a new seed of hope—his Son. Jesus is conceived in heavenly love. He enters the womb of humanity and the Dream comes full term.

Emmanuel is born—"God is with us."

This would bring the prophet's embryonic sermon to full term:

> *"Watch for this—a virgin will get pregnant and bear a*
> *son; they will name him Emmanuel (Hebrew for 'God is*
> *with us')."* [4]

Reflection

Is there a situation in your life where there are too many questions and not enough answers?

In what area of your life is God saying, *"Don't be afraid. Don't hesitate."*?

Do you have any dreams that have been shattered? What new thing is being born in the disappointment?

What impossible, illogical, and incredible thing does God want to do with you?

Prayer

Father,

Like Joseph, I have practical plans. I choose to live a deliberate life. I want everything to fit together and I need to have it all nailed down. But at times, your dreams seem to be at odds with my well conceived, well thought out, well prayed plans. When you choose to give birth to something new, there always seem to be more questions than answers. As you did in Mary, you want to conceive, mature, and give birth to your Son in my life. In me and through Christ, you want to do the impossible. The illogical. The incredible.

During this day, help me hold lightly to my dreams. Assure me that when my dreams die, you're getting ready, in Christ, to give birth to something beautiful. In my disappointment, implant hope. Through the tears, purify my desires. And in the terror of the nightmare, whisper the words,

> *"Don't be afraid. I'm Emmanuel, which means 'God with us.' "*

In the name of your Son I pray.

Amen.

[1]Matthew 1:18 [2]Matthew 1:19 [3]Matthew 1:20-21 [4]Matthew 1:22-23

The Shelter of Provision

"GOD, my shepherd!
I don't need a thing."

Psalm 23:1

David was the shepherd boy who became a king. Though he sat on the throne and wore a crown, his heart never left the green pastures and still waters. The nation of Israel might have been able to take the boy out of the fields but it couldn't take the fields out of the boy.

No surprise then, that when David wrote a psalm praising the character of his God, his memory ran back to the fields of his youth. He uses the metaphor that he knows best to sing his song of praise—sheep and shepherd.

It's a personal psalm—"God, my shepherd."
It's a profession of trust—"don't need a thing." *I shall not want*

As you continue your forty days with Christ, reflect on the following ...

Reflection

Why is it important to personalize the first words of this psalm? *Trust the Lord — The Lord is my shepherd*

In what way are these words a profession of trust?

How has Jesus, the Good Shepherd provided for you?

Day 5:
He Knows My Confusion
Scripture Reading: Luke 2:1-20

Meditation

For a young couple planning marriage, timing is everything. First comes the bended knee—the pledge and the proposal. Next, there are the wedding plans, bridal showers, invitations, and excitement of the engagement. Finally, there's the ceremony, the "I dos", the best wishes from friends and family, the weeklong celebration, and the honeymoon. Then, after all of that, God willing, come the children.

Up until the angel appeared, Mary and Joseph's dreams kept a steady beat. Their plans kept perfect time, not a second too fast or a minute too slow. Their lives marched in step with the turning pages of the wedding planner. Tomorrow never came too early. Yesterday never stayed too late. And Today always knew when to arrive, how long to stay, and when to leave.

But all of this changed when Gabriel suddenly arrived. His announcement blew Mary and Joseph's calendar off the wall and tumbled it fast forward. Its pages flipped months ahead. Heaven's messianic timetable spun this young couple's predictable and planned world around and reset their lives to heaven's time zone.

What's more, Caesar Augustus issued a decree. Of all things, of all the times, the Emperor called for a census of the entire Roman world during the end of Mary's third trimester. Just when she was getting ready to nest, the divine gust of God's plan blew through the mouth of Augustus and knocked her from the safety of her maternal tree. Falling and flailing, she'd have to spread her wings and fly with Joseph to Bethlehem— a three-day journey from Nazareth.

*About that time Caesar Augustus ordered a census to be
taken throughout the Empire. This was the first census
when Quirinius was governor of Syria. Everyone had to
travel to his own ancestral hometown to be accounted for.
So Joseph went from the Galilean town of Nazareth up to
Bethlehem in Judah, David's town, for the census. As a
descendant of David, he had to go there. He went with
Mary, his fiancée who was pregnant.* [1]

Though Caesar intended to keep the Roman Peace through
his imperial order, he has created chaos for the young couple.

*While they were there, the time came for her to give
birth. She gave birth to a son, her firstborn. She wrapped
him in a blanket and laid him in a manger, because
there was no room in the hostel.* [2]

The timing of the census brings turmoil, the turmoil brings
questions, and—when Joseph can't give Mary any logical
answers to the questions—confusion shreds the couple's neat-
ly organized calendar.

*"Joseph, are you sure we're the right couple? Are we going
to the right place? Is this really the right time? Because
all of this seems all so wrong."*

In the midst of the turmoil, Mary and Joseph pray for peace.
In the chaos, they need the calm that can only come from
divine order. In the confusion, they need affirmation.
Somehow, some way, from someone, they need to hear,

*"You are the right couple. You're in the right place.
Don't worry, it is the right time."*

The affirmation comes. God places his stamp of approval on Mary and Joseph. He verifies that Bethlehem, the city of David, is the place. He even validates the timing of Caesar's census. But he doesn't affirm it through kings or priests. He asserts it through those standing on the lowest rung of the social ladder—shepherds.

Though the shepherds are excluded from the everyday events of society, God chooses to give these social outcasts heaven's inclusive message. While watching their flocks at night, an angel of the great company of the heavenly host appears. As he blazes, he trumpets good news.

> *"Don't be afraid. I'm here to announce a great and joyful event that is meant for everybody, worldwide: A Savior has just been born in David's town, a Savior who is Messiah and Master. This is what you're to look for: a baby wrapped in a blanket and lying in a manger."* [3]

After an angelic choir gathers and sings *Gloria in Excelsis Deo*, the shepherds run off to Bethlehem to see this revelation. They've been given a sign. They are to look for a baby wrapped in a blanket and lying in a manger. They go. When they find the baby, they bow in worship. Then they return and spread the word about all that they had heard and seen.

Though dazed, Mary and Joseph are no longer confused. What seemed all so wrong, now feels all so right. Peace has replaced the chaos. In the days, months, and years to come, Mary treasures these moments.

> *Mary kept all these things to herself, holding them dear, deep within herself.* [4]

Maybe it was this treasure that sustained Mary at the foot of the cross. Perhaps, as she watched her son die, she dug deep within herself and unearthed the priceless chest of her memories. When the sword of suffering pierced her spirit, she remembered the precious words of the shepherds.

"We have come because the angel told us that today, for us, there has been born a Savior, Christ the Lord."

Reflection

How does God's plan sometimes confuse you?

When was the last time you thought that when God chose you, he had chosen the wrong person; that he had put you in the wrong place; and did it all at the wrong time?

"Today. For you. A Savior." How does this good news change your life?

What memories of Christ do you hold dear, deep within your heart?

Prayer

Father,

When the Holy Spirit planted the seed of your Son into the womb of Mary, a virgin betrothed to Joseph, you gave birth to chaos. You disrupted a young couple's wedding plans. You altered their timetable. When it came time for Mary to give birth, you uprooted this couple from their comfortable home in Nazareth and relocated them to Bethlehem. Caesar's mouth may have issued the decree but the words behind the edict were yours.

During this day, remind me that, whenever your Son is born in us, he disrupts, interrupts, and radically changes the course of our lives. Though I may be in turmoil, assure me that your Son brings with him peace. In the chaos and confusion of the Christ-life that I live, remind me of the words of the angel,

"Today. For you. A Savior."

Like Mary, may I hide these words deep in my heart, cherish them as priceless treasure, and ponder them daily. It's in the name of your Son, the Prince of Peace, that I pray.

Amen.

1Luke 2:1-5 2Luke 2:6-7 3Luke 2:10-12 4Luke 2:19

Day 6:
He Knows My Terror

Scripture Reading: Matthew 2:1-23

Meditation

As Mary and Joseph settle in Bethlehem, a river of blood flows through Judea. Its headwaters begin at the foot of Herod's throne and its current courses through the small Roman province.

Herod's terror surges through every village surrounding Jerusalem, sweeping away royal foes, friends, and even family members. When a band of scholars from the East bring news of a newborn King of the Jews, Herod's rage is diverted toward King David's town—Bethlehem.

> *After Jesus was born in Bethlehem village, Judah territory—this was during Herod's kingship—a band of scholars arrived in Jerusalem from the East. They asked around, "Where can we find and pay homage to the newborn King of the Jews? We observed a star in the eastern sky that signaled his birth. We're on pilgrimage to worship him."*
>
> *When word of their inquiry got to Herod, he was terrified—and not Herod alone, but most of Jerusalem as well.* [1]

Herod the Great is a puppet king. He's the little big man of Rome's Judean province. Appointed by the Roman senate, he wants to rule Judea alone. He wants to be sole king of the Jews. No competitors. No threats to the throne. When he thought his own family was about to turn on him, he didn't hesitate to draw the blade. He murdered his wife, his three sons, mother-in-law, brother-in-law, and countless others. He has little compassion, no moral conscience, and his fears are stoked hotter by the fuel of his insecurity. And so when the Magi from the East come looking for the one born King of the Jews, Herod and all of Jerusalem are disturbed. All of Jerusalem knows that when Herod is angry, there will be trouble in the province.

Herod sends for the band of scholars. As they come, he sets in place a ruse. He feigns to be a fellow pilgrim worshipper and dispatches the Magi to Bethlehem to look for the newborn King. As they search for the child, Herod begins to sharpen his sword.

> *Herod then arranged a secret meeting with the scholars*
> *from the East. Pretending to be as devout as they were,*
> *he got them to tell him exactly when the birth-announce-*
> *ment star appeared. Then he told them the prophecy*
> *about Bethlehem, and said, "Go find this child. Leave no*
> *stone unturned. As soon as you find him, send word and*
> *I'll join you at once in your worship."* [2]

Guided by the Messianic star in the eastern skies, the wise men set off for Bethlehem. As they travel, their eyes alternate between heaven and earth, sign and destination, promise and fulfillment. They search until star and Savior converge. And when they find their King sitting on Mary's lap, they kneel. They worship. And as the King of the Jews climbs out of his mother's lap and crawls toward them, the Magi open up their dusty bags and present him with gifts: gold, frankincense, and myrrh. For Mary and Joseph, it's like a dream. But the dream is soon to turn into a nightmare.

When Herod realized that the band of Eastern scholars had snuck out of Bethlehem and had taken the long way home, around Jerusalem, he stopped sharpening his sword. Instead, he raised the blade into the sky and released the hounds of hell. But heaven's angelic agents have inside information.

*After the scholars were gone, God's angel showed up
again in Joseph's dream and commanded, "Get up. Take
the child and his mother and flee to Egypt. Stay until
further notice. Herod is on the hunt for this child, and
wants to kill him."*

*Joseph obeyed. He got up, took the child and his mother
under cover of darkness. They were out of town and well
on their way by daylight.* ³

Mary and Joseph know what it's like to live with fear. Ever
since Gabriel appeared, fear has dogged them. It has mixed
itself into their plans. Fear traveled with them to Bethlehem.
It weaved its way into the fiber and fabric of their lives. But
this warning from Gabriel brings much more than fear. It
brings terror—fear pushed to the extreme. It's intense. Fierce.
Violent.

For Mary and Joseph, fear is one thing; terror is another.
Fear frightens; terror overwhelms. Fear is the bad dream in
the middle of the night; terror is waking up to the nightmare
at the break of day. Fear dwells in the realm of possibility; terror moves in, unpacks, and takes up residence in reality. And
reality, according to Gabriel, is that Herod is on his way to kill
the child, and—for good measure—he's planning to kill all of
Bethlehem's boys two years old and under. After today, there
will be no toddling threats to Herod's throne.

As intense as the terror is, God matches it with grace and
then goes beyond it with provision. He supplies to the
extreme. To a blue collar, lower class carpenter with a new
wife and a toddler to feed, he lavishes gold, frankincense, and
myrrh. These are gifts from the hand of God, wrapped and
delivered by the men of the East: resources aplenty to help a
family on the run. They can go anywhere, at any moment, and
stay for any length of time.

Along the way, God provides an angel who maps out the exact route and gives an up-to-date account of current events. When the angel says, "Get up and go," they go. When he says, "Stay," the family pitches its tent. When he says, "Return," they pack up and head home.

> *Later, when Herod died, God's angel appeared in a dream to Joseph in Egypt: "Up, take the child and his mother and return to Israel. All those out to murder the child are dead."* [4]

When terror sends its assassins, heaven dispatches angels. Providence guides. Grace supplies. And peace pitches its tent along the way.

Reflection

What would it be like to have someone hunting your child in order to kill him? Hunting you?

When was the last time you experienced terror—intense, overwhelming fear?

If fear is a bad dream in the middle of the night, what is your waking nightmare? What brings you terror?

How has God protected your life?

Prayer

Father,

Your Son was the true King of the Jews. Though he came as a Prince of Peace, he was a threat to kings and kingdoms. Herod tried to kill him. Through Pilate, Israel rejected, betrayed, and demanded his crucifixion. Rome crowned him with a crown of thorns, nailed him to a tree like a criminal, and pierced his side. But on the third day, your Son rose victorious and was crowned the Lord of heaven and earth, the King of kings. All along, heaven had shielded salvation's plans.

During this day, send Divine Providence to guard my family. When terror sends its assassins, dispatch legions of angels to intervene. When you tell me to pack, hurry, and leave in the middle of the night—show me where to go and remind me how you've provided in advance for the journey. When forced to relocate, assure me that you have gone ahead and pitched a tent of peace. And when it's time to return, give me a clear sign that danger has passed. In every moment of every day, keep me one step ahead of and one step away from the reach of terror. It's in Christ's name that I pray.

Amen.

[1]Matthew 2:1-3 [2]Matthew 2:7-8 [3]Matthew 2:13-14 [4]Matthew 2:19-20

Day 7:
He Knows My Panic

Scripture Reading: Luke 2:41-52

Meditation

A mother's greatest joy is holding her baby close. But there comes a day when she has to open her arms and let him go. It's a moment when she finds herself suddenly looking up at her son, not down. Suddenly she realizes that he's no longer her little boy. When that day comes, she shakes her head. She sheds a tear and sighs,

"When did my baby grow up?"

For Mary, that day has come.

Slowly, over time, Jesus has grown—infant to toddler, toddler to preadolescent, and preadolescent to young man. His development has been steady, almost imperceptible to someone who's been with him every day. Each year he grows a couple of inches. Every month he puts on a couple of pounds. Day after day, his hair grows longer. All the while, his character is growing.

One moment he's a tiny baby wrapped in a blanket and cradled in his mother's arms. The next, he's an energetic, active adolescent: too big to sit on his mother's lap, too busy for Mary to keep an eye on his every move, and too independent to report in and tell his mom where he's been, what he's doing, or where he's going. Mary's little boy has grown up and it all seemed to happen so fast.

Jesus is now twelve years old and he's soon to become a "son of the covenant." In a few months, he'll have his bar mitzvah. He'll pass from being a boy to a man and be considered an adult in the Jewish community. He'll take on all of the moral and religious duties of Judaism. For the past couple of years, he's been preparing for and looking forward to this moment. He's attended all of the annual Jerusalem festivals with his parents.

He's celebrated Passover. He knows all about the sacrificial lamb, the blood on the doorposts, the angel who passed over, and the exodus out of Egypt. Fifty days after Passover, after the wheat had been harvested, he returned to Jerusalem to celebrate the one-day festival of Pentecost.

In the autumn, he returned once again for the Feast of Tabernacles. He helped his father build a booth outside of Jerusalem. For eight days, they tented with the rest of the pilgrims as they remembered the forty years spent wandering in the wilderness. During that feast, Jesus celebrated the provisions of the Father: the manna, the water from the rock, the pillar of fire by night and the cloud by day. Throughout his life, his mother and father have faithfully attended all of these festivals. This year is no different.

> *Every year Jesus' parents traveled to Jerusalem for the Feast of Passover. When he was twelve years old, they went up as they always did for the Feast. When it was over and they left for home, the child Jesus stayed behind in Jerusalem, but his parents didn't know it.* [1]

It's Passover and a sea of pilgrims floods Jerusalem. The Holy City swells with strangers. The current of the crowd could easily sweep a young boy away from his family. Mary tells Jesus to stay close and to hang on to his father's hand. If they get separated, Joseph tells him to meet them on the steps of the temple court.

When the Feast is over, the tide of travelers leaves Jerusalem but Jesus stays behind. His parents, thinking he was traveling with family or friends from Nazareth, didn't know it. It's only after a day of travel that Mary and Joseph notice that Jesus is missing.

> *Thinking he was somewhere in the company of pilgrims, they journeyed for a whole day and then began looking for him among relatives and neighbors. When they didn't find him, they went back to Jerusalem looking for him.* [2]

Panic engulfs Mary. Frantic, she turns to Joseph,

> *"I thought he was with you."*

She runs toward the tents of her relatives, calling out his name as she goes. On the way she stops every friend, every relative, every neighbor asking,

> *"Has anyone seen Jesus?*
> *When was the last time you saw him? Where?"*

No one has seen Jesus.

The last time anyone remembers seeing Jesus was when they were all in the Temple courts. But by now it's night and it's not safe to travel after the sun goes down. Mary paces till the sun rises. Fear keeps her awake. Terror fills her thoughts. Dread prays for the dawn.

At first light, Mary and Joseph head back to Jerusalem. They travel a full day but are forced to wait through another night before they can start to search for Jesus.

The next day they found him in the Temple seated among the teachers, listening to them and asking questions. The teachers were all quite taken with him, impressed with the sharpness of his answers. But his parents were not impressed; they were upset and hurt. [3]

Relief! Jesus is safe. Three days separated from his parents and no harm has come to him. But after Mary's long embrace, Joseph's ruffling of Jesus' hair, and a parental sigh of relief, comes a mother's scolding finger.

"Young man, why have you done this to us? Your father and I have been half out of our minds looking for you." [4]

Jesus gives no adolescent excuse. He doesn't even offer an apology. Instead, he answers his mother's question with a question of his own.

"Why were you looking for me? Didn't you know that I had to be here, dealing with the things of my Father?" But they had no idea what he was talking about. [5]

In the midst of his mother's panic, Jesus explains that he was dealing with the things of his Father: heavenly business.

This was the day that Mary, the mother of God, had to open her arms and let her son go. It wasn't until later, when she fell at the foot of the cross, that she realized why she had to let him go. She had to open her arms so that he could open his ...

to the nails,
to forgiveness,
to a world frantic in its sin.

Years later, on the cross, her little boy would still be about his Father's business.

Reflection

When you were a child, how did you throw your parents into a panic?

What does it feel like to be in a panic—half out of your mind?

Have you ever been hurt or upset by Jesus' actions? When? How?

When was the last time Jesus responded, *"Why were you looking for me? Didn't you know I had to be here dealing with the things of my Father?"*

Prayer

Father,

Though Jesus was your Son, he grew in body and matured in spirit. He was the Son of God and yet he was just like any other Jewish boy. He ran for hours. He played all day with his friends. As he approached adolescence, he spread his wings of independence and flew off from his mother's nest. When Jesus was a child, his mother held him close like a baby bird. But when he was about to become a man, she knew that she had to open her arms and let him go. He had to soar toward the things of heaven: the cross, forgiveness, and eternal life.

During this day, help me see that Jesus is still about his Father's business. When I panic and wonder where the Son of Mary is, give me peace. When I can't seem to find him in the crowd, assure me that he is in his Father's house. When I'm upset and hurt—out of my mind because I don't know where Jesus is—remind me that he is present, with me always, still dealing with the things of heaven. It's in the Son of Mary's name that I pray.

Amen.

[1]Luke 2:41-43 [2]Luke 2:44-45 [3]Luke 2:46-48 [4]Luke 2:48 [5]Luke 2:49-50

Day 8:
He Knows My Plea

Scripture Reading: John 4:43-54

Meditation

The village of Cana is still abuzz about Jesus' last visit.

They all remember the wedding with the heavenly wine. But it was only after the wedding that they found out what had really happened. The groom had miscalculated—more guests than wine.

Mary, Jesus' mother, had whispered the news in his ear and he intervened. He changed the water that was stored in six stone jars into the best vintage the village guests had ever had. And no one was the wiser until after the wedding. That was the first miraculous sign Jesus performed in Cana of Galilee. He revealed his glory and his disciples believed in him.

But Jesus is a prophet without honor.

The last time he paid a visit to his hometown of Nazareth, his childhood friends showed him no respect. His teaching offended them. His Messianic claims infuriated them. When he declared that he was the fulfillment of prophecy, they said,

"Enough is enough."

The very ones that he grew up with grabbed him by the arm, drove him out of town, took him to the brow of the hill on which the village was built, and tried to throw him off of the edge of the cliff in order to kill him. Miraculously, he walked right through the crowd and went on his way. He left Galilee and went on to Jerusalem where he performed many signs.

When Jesus returned to Galilee from Jerusalem, crowds rushed toward him. But when they came, they came looking for a miracle worker, not a Messiah. They wanted signs and wonders, mystical manifestations and feats of power, promising potions, remedies, and elixirs. They wanted a sideshow, not a Savior.

When Jesus sees the crowd, he sighs. So many signs and yet there has been so little faith. Every healing was a fingerprint left by the hand of God; every miracle a mark of divine mercy; and every wonder a footprint—heaven's Son is walking among his creation. God is in Galilee.

Though Jesus has posted many signs along the way, the crowds haven't followed down the road that leads to faith. Those in Galilee are satisfied with the sights and sounds of the Messianic journey but they've forgotten that there is a destination. Someone—the Messiah—is waiting for them at the end of the road.

> *Now, Jesus knew well from experience that a prophet is not respected in the place where he grew up. So when he arrived in Galilee, the Galileans welcomed him, but only because they were impressed with what he had done in Jerusalem during the Passover Feast, not that they really had a clue about who he was or what he was up to.* [1]

The crowd that greets Jesus in Galilee doesn't have a clue as to who he really is. Throngs of people welcome him but they don't care about what he's up to. They're not interested in Jesus the person. They're interested in Jesus the *performer*. They want a good show, a spectacle, something to write home about. Jesus is amazed at their unbelief. And so he makes up his mind; there will be no more signs in Galilee, no show in Cana.

To the east of Cana is a village on the Sea of Galilee, Capernaum. There a royal official in Herod's Court has just heard that Jesus, the miracle worker, has returned. The official's son is sick and close to death. He runs to Jesus and pleads with him to come to Capernaum in order to heal his son. The official's plea is earnest and urgent. It's a matter of life and death for his son. When he comes to Jesus, he begs for a morsel of mercy but Jesus doesn't even break off a crumb. Instead, he puts him off with blunt word,

> *"Unless you people are dazzled by a miracle, you refuse to believe."*
>
> *But the court official wouldn't be put off. "Come down! It's life or death for my son."* [2]

The father persists. He perseveres. He is tenacious and Jesus honors his plea. But Jesus wants to see if this father's faith has any legs. Jesus assures him that his son is alive and then orders him to return home. He asks the father to start walking. He gives him no proof, no evidence, no guarantee except the bare word of his promise. Jesus asks the father to turn and run toward home—in faith.

> *Jesus simply replied, "Go home. Your son lives."*
>
> *The man believed the bare word Jesus spoke and headed home. On his way back, his servants intercepted him and announced, "Your son lives!"* [3]

The father walks the long road home. Every step he takes leaves an imprint of faith. Each stride is a statement of belief. Every mile he travels is a testimony. Jesus had honored the royal official's plea and then the Master had asked him to get a firm grip on a strong promise and sent him on his way.

Halfway home, the royal official's servants intercept him. As they run toward him, they wave their hands in the air and shout,

"It's a miracle!
    Your boy's alive! He's all right!"

The father asks his servants when his son began to feel better. They reply,

"The fever broke yesterday afternoon at one o'clock."
The father knew that that was the very moment Jesus
had said, "Your son lives."

That clinched it. Not only he but his entire household
believed. [4]

The timing is too perfect to be coincidence. Yesterday, when Jesus spoke, there was no delay. He wasn't deterred by distance. He spoke and it was done. Jesus gave the word and directed the father to begin the long walk home. Faith led this man and his household right into the kingdom of God. In the miracle, Messiah had been revealed.

No sideshow, only a Savior.

Reflection

When was the last time you pleaded with Jesus, *"Come! It's a matter of life and death!"?*

In what way is Jesus asking you to start walking? What bare word of promise is Jesus asking you to hold on to?

What does it feel like to leave the presence of Christ without any evidence?

How has God divinely orchestrated the events of your life? (Occasions when there is no question in your mind that Christ intervened. No thought of happenstance. No coincidence.)

Prayer

Father,

Your Son was a prophet without honor: divinity walking the earth without human applause. He came to his own yet his own rejected him. They embraced his miracles but they shunned him. They came looking for signs and wonders, mystical manifestations and feats of power, promising potions, remedies, and elixirs: not a Messiah. They turned Jesus into a sideshow and forgot that he was a Savior.

During this day, give me a faith that takes your Son at his word. May I come longing for an encounter with the Messiah and not demanding a miracle. When I beg for mercy, place grace in my hands. When your Son says, *"Go,"* make my feet move toward home. As I walk, close my hands tightly and help me grip the bare promise of his Word. And when good news intercepts me along the way, may my heart leap, my mind reel, and my soul embrace the Messiah behind the miracle. May Jesus the Christ be a prophet with honor in my life. It's in his name that I plead.

Amen.

[1]John 4:44-45 [2]John 4:48-49 [3]John 4:50-51 [4]John 4:52-53

Day 9:
He Knows My Helplessness

Scripture Reading: John 5:1-15

Meditation

The pool of Bethesda is where the angel of the Lord swims.

Popular belief has it that whoever is the first to jump into the pool when the angel splashes is the one who would be cured of whatever disease he had. But there is only one miracle per angelic outing. The first one in is the only one healed.

Day after day, hundreds of disabled people—the blind, the diseased, and the crippled—wait for the stirring of the waters. They crowd in and camp out in one of the five alcoves that surround the pool. Minute by minute, they look for any ripple caused by the brush of angel wings. Any undulation. A swirl.

When the angel comes, he gives no notice. He has no set schedule. He could come at any moment. Those gathered around the pool know that, if you want to be cured, you have to be vigilant, ready, and fast. You can't be late. Any waves in the water and you have to beat everyone else into the pool.

For thirty-eight years a man lying by the edge of the pool has always been late. Whenever the angel stirred the waters, he's been too slow. Somebody else always seems to splash his or her way to wholeness before he can even get his toe in the water.

What's made matters worse is that his friends and family, anyone that could or would help, have abandoned him. The paralytic is alone by the side of the pool.

He's helpless—unable to get into the pool. He can see the water ripple but his legs anchor him to his bedroll. Healing always comes to someone else.

He's hopeless—after thirty-eight years of missing his chance to swim with the angel, he's no longer willing to try. He's so close to healing and yet so far from a miracle.

He's become heartless—unfeeling, insensitive, and dead to the joys of others. His emotions, like his legs, are paralyzed. He's become numb to those around him and numb to God. When someone else is healed, his heart is further hardened.

It's this man that Jesus decides to help.

> *One man had been an invalid there for thirty-eight years. When Jesus saw him stretched out by the pool and knew how long he had been there, he said, "Do you want to get well?"*
>
> *The sick man said, "Sir, when the water is stirred, I don't have anybody to put me in the pool. By the time I get there, somebody else is already in."* [1]

For as many years as the paralytic has been lying next to the pool, he has connected healing with the stirring of the waters. But today, Jesus wants to stir his soul. When the paralytic sees Jesus, he makes no request. There is no plea for healing. And Jesus doesn't reach down and offer him a hand up, or give him a crutch, or even help him into the pool. Instead, Jesus gives him a command.

> *"Get up, take your bedroll, start walking." The man was healed on the spot. He picked up his bedroll and walked off. That day happened to be the Sabbath.* [2]

What Jesus asks is impossible. On his own, the man is unable to comply. But in, with, and underneath the command, Jesus gives power. The paralytic is healed on the spot. He straightens his legs. He stands up, picks up his bedroll, and walks off. And he doesn't even have to get wet.

But with the healing comes controversy.

> *The Jews stopped the healed man and said, "It's the Sabbath. You can't carry your bedroll around. It's against the rules."* [3]

When the Jews see the one time paralytic carrying his bedroll, they don't rejoice with the man; they rebuke him. Technically he's not breaking the Law of Moses but he is violating the strict regulations established by the religious authorities: no load carrying of any kind on the Sabbath. Just healed or not, rules are rules.

> *But he told them, "The man who made me well told me to. He said, 'Take your bedroll and start walking.'"*
>
> *They asked, "Who gave you the order to take it up and start walking?" But the healed man didn't know, for Jesus had slipped away into the crowd.* [4]

Again Jesus takes the initiative. Earlier, he had found the paralytic lying next to the pool. Now he finds him in the Temple about to give thanks.

*"You look wonderful! You're well! Don't return to a
sinning life or something worse might happen."* [5]

A few hours ago, Jesus straightened his legs; now he wants
to strengthen his soul. Whether it's paralyzed limbs or numb
hearts, Jesus finds and helps the helpless. The healed paralytic
presents his thank offering and skips away singing a psalm.

*"God, you did everything you promised,
    and I'm thanking you with all my heart.
You pulled me from the brink of death,
    my feet from the cliff-edge of doom.
Now I stroll at leisure with God
    in the sunlit fields of life."* [6]

Reflection

In what areas of your life do you feel like you're helpless? What pool are you waiting for Christ to stir?

When has Jesus asked you to do something that you were powerless to do? How has he given you the power to do it?

In what ways has a work of Christ in your life caused controversy in your world?

When you're in the Temple, what thank offering do you bring? What Psalm do you sing?

Prayer

Father,

Your Son is the Savior who takes the initiative. He finds hurting people, involves himself in their lives, cures their bodies, and cares for their souls. When it comes to the needs of the powerless, he pays no attention to manmade rules. The dignity of the individual is more important than the dictates of the law. Sabbath or no Sabbath, your Son is going to do his work and give the helpless rest.

During this day, Jesus, find me where I lay. If I'm helpless and unable to move, say the word. Give the command and make me strong. If I'm hopeless and unwilling to try, breathe into me a reason to dream. If I'm heartless, unfeeling towards the joys of others and numb toward you, soften my heart and stir my soul. And after you work, may you find me in the Temple, offering thanks, and singing a psalm. It's in your name that I pray.

Amen.

1John 5:5-7 2John 5:8-9 3John 5:10 4John 5:11-13 5John 5:14 6Psalm 56:12-13

Day 10:
He Knows My Loss

Scripture Reading: Luke 7:11-23

Meditation

For the widow from the village Nain, the death of her only son represents loss upon loss.

As her son's funeral procession makes it way toward the village cemetery, the widow carries a double burden. She's walked the path from her home to the graveyard once before. Not long ago, she sorrowfully followed her husband's coffin. Now her son's pallbearers lead the way.

Tears for her son mix with new tears for her husband. Grief is revisited. As she wails for one, she weeps for the other. Grief is multiplied. There is no longer a man in her family. No husband to provide for her. No son to protect her. Neither will return at the end of the day, sit at her table, share a meal, and talk until heavy eyes and a weary body give way. Her heart mirrors her home: empty, hollow, so much room and yet no one to fill the space.

She's alone—husbandless and childless.

The second walk to the cemetery is worse than the first. Though the death of her husband was a violent blow, at least her son was there to help absorb the pain. As they walked to the graveyard, he was there by her side. Together they wept. Together they said their "goodbyes." And when the funeral was over they walked home, together. Theirs was shared loss, shared sorrow, and shared comfort.

Today she walks the path alone. she walks the path alone. But her son's funeral procession will never reach the cemetery. It will end at the village gate.

Not long after that, Jesus went to the village Nain. His disciples were with him, along with quite a large crowd. As they approached the village gate, they met a funeral procession—a woman's only son was being carried out for burial. And the mother was a widow. When Jesus saw her, his heart broke. He said to her, "Don't cry." [1]

When Jesus sees the sobbing widow drowning in her grief, buoyed up only by the arms of her friends, he jumps into the depths her sorrow. He suffers with her. Her tears become his tears. Her pain is his pain. Her loss is his loss. His heart breaks and floods with compassion. As he wipes the tears from her cheeks, he whispers softly in her ear,

"Don't cry."

Jesus' words are more than a whisper of solace. They intend more than a one-time, well-meaning phrase of comfort or an awkward, yet authentic, attempt at consolation. His words are a promise—lights perforating the darkness, a blazing foreshadow of the miraculous, a revelation of things soon to come. When Jesus speaks, there is substance behind his words. Life. Hope.

Then he went over and touched the coffin. The pallbearers stopped. He said, "Young man, I tell you: Get up." [2]

As Jesus touches the coffin, he risks defilement. The Law clearly says,

Anyone out in the open field who touches a corpse, whether dead from violent or natural causes, or a human bone or a grave is unclean for seven days. [3]

But when Jesus touches the coffin, the only thing that's defiled is death.

The dead son sat up and began talking. Jesus presented him to his mother. [4]

Jesus does more than wipe away the widow's tears; he goes to grief's source and stops the flow. He dives deep, down to the spring of her pain. He finds the dear one that is lost and does battle with the legions of Hades. Freeing the son of the widow from the grip of death, he presents him back to his mother. No more tears.

A quiet awe hovers over the crowd. The only sound comes from the coffin. Still dressed in his burial clothes, the resurrected son sits up, turns, and begins to talk to his mother.

They all realized they were in a place of holy mystery, that God was at work among them. They were quietly worshipful—and then noisily grateful, calling out among themselves, "God is back, looking to the needs of his people!" The news of Jesus spread all through the country. [5]

It's evident to the crowd that God is present. He's active, working among his people. Help from heaven has come. God is walking among his creation and he's looking to the needs of his people. Jesus has to be the One—the Messiah that Israel has been waiting for.

In him,

> *The blind see,*
> *The lame walk,*
> *Lepers are cleansed,*
> *The deaf hear,*
> *The dead are raised,*
> *The wretched of the earth*
>   *have God's salvation hospitality extended to them.* [6]

Whatever the loss, the Messiah's heart breaks. Pushed by compassion, he jumps into the depths of sorrow. He suffers with those who hurt and shares their pain. And then, in the midst of the tears, he gives a gentle stroke of his hand and whispers a promise,

"Don't cry."

Reflection

What loss are you mourning? When Jesus looks at your life, what makes his heart break?

How has Jesus shown you his compassion? How has he whispered, *"Don't cry"?*

What work of Christ has made you say, *"God is back, looking to the needs of his people"?*

Describe your *"place of holy mystery"*—a place where you are *"quietly worshipful and then noisily grateful"?*

Prayer

Father,

Your Son is a Savior full of compassion. Whenever one of your children experiences a loss, Jesus' heart breaks. He cries tears. He shares in the pain. And in the loss he says, *"Don't cry."* He offers words of comfort that drowning hearts can hold on to because *in, with,* and *under* the words is a promise: he is a Savior who is actively at work, looking out for the needs of his people.

During this day, I need to feel the hand of Christ stroke my cheek. I so desperately need to hear him whisper in my ear, *"Don't cry."* I have many losses and they bring me great pain. Assure me that, in Jesus, help from heaven has come—God is looking out for my needs. And when he touches my life, may I recognize that moment as a place of holy mystery—God is working. Help me be quietly worshipful and then noisily grateful. It's in your Son's name that I pray.

Amen.

[1]Luke 7:11-13 [2]Luke 7:14 [3]Numbers 19:16 [4]Luke 7:15 [5]Luke 7:16-17 [6]Luke 7:22

The Shelter of Peace

"You have bedded me down in lush meadows, you find me quiet pools to drink from"

Psalm 23:2

Peace. The very sound of the word is soothing to the soul. It's a quiet word not easily heard above the clatter of the world's daily chaos. It never shouts over the madness; it whispers calm into it.

When the world overwhelms the heart, the peace of the Good Shepherd beds the weary down in lush meadows. He leads the thirsty to quiet pools. He sings nighttime lullabies and says bedtime prayers. He tucks the frightened child, shaking in all of us, tightly into our bed—safe, secure, and at rest for the night.

In the chaos of your forty days with Christ, reflect on the following ...

Reflection

What part of your soul needs soothing?

What quiet words do you need to hear from Christ in your noisy world?

During the last week, how has the Good Shepherd brought you peace?

Day 11:
He Knows My Unbelief

Scripture Reading: Mark 9:14-32

Meditation

When a child is in constant pain and a father's persistent prayers go unanswered, doubt begins to tear faith apart. The father who comes to Jesus' disciples with his demon-possessed son has faith, but it's a faith intermixed with unbelief. And right now, unbelief is slowly taking over the lion's share of this father's heart.

A small part of his heart still believes that God is powerful and merciful, that he does intervene and can do the impossible, that he, too, has a father's heart that beats fast for his children. But when the demon attacks his son, this God seems to sit passively in his heaven. He appears to be deaf to prayers and either too busy or unable to offer a healing and helping hand. With every seizure of his son, the father's faith is shaken and unbelief begins to lay a firm foundation.

This struggle of faith is nothing new. From childhood, a demon of Satan has stalked his son. The evil spirit has robbed his boy of speech. It has ravaged his body, thrown him into the fire countless times, and tried to drown him. When the tormenting demon comes, all this father can do is panic and pray. The son is defenseless; the father is powerless. Though the father longs to help his son, he can't stop the attacks. He can't calm the convulsions. He can't take away the pain. And when the sadistic spirit finally leaves, the father can't even promise his son that it's over. There is no assurance that hell's henchman won't come back. There may be more to be afraid of.

For this father, the days have been long and the nights even longer. The thief that ravages the boy's body has also robbed the father of his energy. His son needs constant care, countless prayers. A continual watch has to be manned for the next attack. The battle has been so long, so hard, and the demon is so close to victory. It has bereaved the father of his hope and deprived him of all of his parental dreams.

When his son cut his first tooth, the demon ground and gnashed it. When his toddler raised his foot to take his first steps, the evil one that had invaded the boy's body seized him. It threw him to the ground and thrashed him around until he foamed at the mouth. When it was time for him to utter his first words, there was no "Abba", only a growl. When the attacks come, they are so violent that the father can't get near his son. He can't hold him. He can't stroke his hair or wipe away the tears. When he asks ...

"What's wrong?
Where does it hurt? What's going on?"

... his son can't answer. All his son can do is moan. With each moan and every unanswered prayer, the father's faith exits and unbelief enters.

But though unbelief is moving in, it hasn't yet evicted this father's faith. Miraculous news has just come from Galilee. A man named Jesus and twelve of his followers have been going from village to village, teaching, preaching, healing the sick and driving out many demons. It is said that these men even have authority over evil spirits.

Upon hearing the news, the father immediately picks up his boy and runs to the village. When he arrives, he doesn't find Jesus but he does find nine of the twelve disciples. He pleads with them to heal his son. He begs for pity.

The disciples surround the boy. Just like every other exorcism they've performed, they stretch out their hands and command the spirit to come out. But this time the evil spirit doesn't exit. Instead, through the boy's shriek, the demon scoffs at the disciples. To show them that he's still alive and kicking, the demon grabs hold of the boy and throws him thrashing to the ground.

As the boy begins to shake and foam at the mouth, a large crowd hurriedly gathers. The teachers of the law disregard the plight of the boy; instead, they use his pain to mock the impotency of the disciples. Tempers flare and an argument begins. Just as things are about to come to blows, Jesus, Peter, James, and John enter the village, straight from the Mount of Transfiguration. When those in the crowd see Jesus, they are overwhelmed with wonder and run to greet him. As they encircle him, Jesus asks,

"What's going on? What's all the commotion?" [1]

The father in the crowd answered,

"Teacher, I brought my mute son, made speechless by a demon, to you. Whenever it seizes him, it throws him to the ground. He foams at the mouth, grinds his teeth, and goes stiff as a board. I told your disciples, hoping they could deliver him, but they couldn't." [2]

Jesus shakes his head in bitter disappointment and rebukes the unbelief of his disciples.

"What a generation! No sense of God! How many times do I have to go over these things? How much longer do I have to put up with this? Bring the boy here." [3]

The disciples bring the boy to Jesus but as soon as the demon sees the Savior, it throws the boy into a seizure. Quickly, Jesus catches the eye of the father and asks him what's wrong with the boy and how long this has been going on. The father answers,

> *"Ever since he was a little boy. Many times it pitches him into fire or the river to do away with him. If you can do anything, do it. Have a heart and help us!"*
>
> *Jesus said, "If? There are no 'ifs' among believers. Anything can happen."*
>
> *No sooner were the words out of his mouth than the father cried, "Then I believe. Help me with my doubts!"* [4]

Jesus sparks belief in the father. He douses his doubts and ignites hope. He kindles and fuels faith until divine possibilities begin to blaze. Taking the boy, Jesus rebukes the evil spirit, commanding the tormenter to leave and demanding that he never enter the child again.

The demon violently convulses the boy one last time and then he leaves, never to enter again. But as he leaves, the boy's body goes limp—corpselike. The crowd thinks the boy is dead but Jesus takes him by the hand and gives him back to his father. Alive. Vibrant. Free.

Jesus has just given an unbelieving generation an undeniable sign. He has freed an imprisoned child from demonic chains and he has helped a father with a fragile faith overcome his doubts.

Reflection

Depression - lonliness

Who or what is attacking your family? What fears do you have for your family? How are they affecting your faith in Christ?

How have you said to Christ, *"If you can do anything, do it. Have a heart and help us!"?*

Write a prayer to Jesus.

Begin by saying, "I do believe that you can ..."

Finish the prayer by saying, "I'm having a hard time believing ... help me with my doubts."

Prayer

Father,

You know what it's like to stand and watch your son suffer. Satan tempted him. His own people tortured and crucified him. When he suffered, he cried, "Father" and begged for your mercy. Though he was your son, you let him endure the full wrath of hell's demons. He went to the cross and entered the tomb but rose on the third day. He conquered sin, death, and the power of the devil.

During this day, take pity on me and help me. When the evil one attacks those I love, give me faith in order that I might believe; strength so that I might endure; courage so that I might fight; love in order that I might comfort others; peace so that I might rest; hope in order that I might continue; joy so that I can worship; patience in order that I might wait; and persistence so that I might always pray. I do believe that everything is possible with, in, and through your Son but I need your help to overcome my unbelief. It's in his name that I pray.

Amen.

1Mark 9:16 2Mark 9:17-18 3Mark 9:19 4Mark 9:21-24

Day 12:
He Knows My Faith

Scripture Reading: Luke 7:1-10

Meditation

Soldiers understand authority.

They live and move under the chain of command. When their commander says "Go," they go. When he says "Come," they come. When he says "Do this," they do it double time. In the chain of command, every order is a link of life. Break the chain and someone could die. In the military, authority is respected. Orders are the norm and unquestioned obedience is expected.

The centurion stationed at Capernaum leads one hundred soldiers, but while he leads, he also serves. He's under the authority of another. As a leader, he knows that with authority comes power, with power comes responsibility, and with responsibility comes a charge to do what's moral, noble, and right.

The centurion has heard about the power of Jesus. Many have told him that this teacher from Galilee has unrivaled spiritual authority. They say that, with a single command, he can make demons flee, the lame skip, fevers break, and the leprous clean. When enemy forces come face-to-face with Jesus, sickness surrenders and evil spirits abandon their posts. Even death waves a white flag and releases its prisoners.

After hearing all of this, the centurion asks the elders of Capernaum to go, find, and plead with Jesus to come and heal his servant.

For days his servant has been close to death. Every doctor has been called. Every medication has been tried. Every friend has been asked to pray and yet the servant is about to die. He's more than a domestic hand, more than a stable boy or an armor bearer. He's an invaluable aide, a priceless part of the centurion's life. He's not just another hired hand; he's a cherished part of the centurion's family.

The centurion's hope is that what's true in the realm of Caesar's legions of command might also be true in the realm of the spiritual forces of evil.

> *When he heard Jesus was back, he sent leaders from the Jewish community asking him to come and heal his servant. They came to Jesus and urged him to do it, saying, "He deserves this. He loves our people. He even built our meeting place."*
>
> *Jesus went with them. [1]*

Though the centurion is a Gentile, the elders of Capernaum think highly of him. When they come to Jesus, they praise the centurion for his generous support and aid in the building of the local synagogue. They also applaud his authentic affection for the nation of Israel.

For a representative of an occupying power, he's well respected. He's well liked. More than that, he's genuinely accepted by the elders of Capernaum and even called a "friend." In the elders' opinion, if anyone deserves to have Jesus come under his roof, it's this man.

Jesus is persuaded by their plea. He goes with the elders and they make their way to the centurion's house. When the centurion sees Jesus start down the path that leads to his house, he quickly sends another set of friends. These friends don't plead with Jesus to hurry or beg him to run; instead, they ask

Jesus to stop. They tell him to just give the command and then they ask him to return to his in-progress itinerary. It was faith that dispatched the invitation and now it's faith that takes it back.

> *When he was still quite far from the house, the captain sent friends to tell him, "Master, you don't have to go to all this trouble. I'm not that good a person, you know. I'd be embarrassed for you to come to my house, even embarrassed to come to you in person. Just give the order and my servant will get well. I'm a man under orders; I also give orders. I tell one soldier, 'Go,' and he goes; another, 'Come,' and he comes; my slave, 'Do this,' and he does it."* [2]

"Jesus, just give the order." It's a Gentile soldier's public submission to Jesus' authority. The request catches everyone by surprise. The elders who had pleaded the centurion's case and begged Jesus to come stand stunned. The gawkers who follow in the crowd behind are disappointed. The disciples are stupefied. Jesus, however, stands amazed. He's thrilled to find such great faith.

This is what Jesus has been looking for in Israel: someone who would believe, trust, and take him at his word. Up to now, the only thing that has amazed Jesus is his own people's unbelief.

> *Taken aback, Jesus addressed the accompanying crowd: "I've yet to come across this kind of simple trust anywhere in Israel, the very people who are supposed to know about God and how he works." When the messengers got back home, they found the servant up and well.* [3]

Like a commander in the battlefield, Jesus gives the order. At his command, the angels don their armor; mercy, grace, and truth take up their swords; and the legions of heaven begin to march against the forces of evil.

Jesus orders *"Believe,"* and faith begins to fight.
He charges *"Go,"* and the servant's disease deserts the battlefield.
He commands *"Come,"* and reinforcements move in—life, strength, and hope.

Jesus says the word and faith turns into sight.

Reflection

How does Christ's authority affect your life?

In what ways are you unworthy to have Christ come under your roof?

What is Christ amazed about in your life?

Write a prayer. Begin with the words, "Jesus, just give the order and ..."

Prayer

Father,

You have given your Son all authority in heaven and on earth. He is well aware that with that authority comes power; with that power comes responsibility; and with that responsibility comes a heavenly charge to do what's moral, noble, and right. As your Son marched toward the cross, he advanced his kingdom. Every illness was a battle, every healing a victory. As he walked out of the tomb, he conquered sin and vanquished death. He subjugated the plans and power of the evil one.

During this day, create faith in me—a faith that will send for you, a faith that will stop you on your way and say it's not worthy for you to come under its roof, a faith that will amaze you. Each day, may I live under your authority. I want to be your valued servant. When you say "Go," make my legs run. When you say "Come," make my heart beat fast. When you say "Do this," make my hands move. And when Satan tries to ravage my soul, pillage my hope, and attack those I love, give me the faith to say, *"Jesus, just give the order."* It's in your Son's name that I pray.

Amen.

[1]Luke 7:3-6 [2]Luke 7:6-8 [3]Luke 7:9-10

Day 13:
He Knows My Desire To Be First
Scripture Reading: Mark 9:30-37; 10:32-45

Meditation

The road to Jerusalem leads to a cross but Jesus walks the path anyway. Though they pledge their allegiance to the Master, the disciples, however, want to go their own way. They want to walk the way of glory. They run after the crown and away from the cross.

As they make their way to Jerusalem, Jesus tries to explain to his disciples what is about to happen.

> *Back on the road, they set out for Jerusalem. Jesus had a head start on them, and they were following, puzzled and not just a little afraid. He took the Twelve and began again to go over what to expect next. "Listen to me carefully. We're on our way up to Jerusalem. When we get there, the Son of Man will be betrayed to the religious leaders and scholars. They will sentence him to death. Then they will hand him over to the Romans, who will mock and spit on him, give him the third degree, and kill him. After three days he will rise alive."* [1]

But Jesus' predictions about his Passion are difficult for his disciples to accept. Betrayal. Humiliation. Murder. These thoughts are abhorrent, unthinkable. Such things are hard to believe and even more loathsome to embrace.

The disciples have it set in their minds that the road to Jerusalem should lead to a throne, not a cross. The political climate is right. All of Jerusalem is ready for a Messianic king and Jesus' followers are determined that he is destined for a coronation, not a crucifixion. The disciples reject his words and spurn the course to the cross. Instead, they run after dreams of kingdom crowns.

As they walk toward Jerusalem, the disciples plot ways to leapfrog themselves over their brothers and up the political pecking order. Each of them is planning to rule. Power. Prestige. Places of honor. These are the perks that come to those who sit at the right and at the left of the Messiah. But there are only two seats next to the throne of glory. In the kingdom, positions on the messianic cabinet are limited and the Father is the only one who can assign them.

Two of the disciples, James and John, come up to Jesus and whisper a request,

> *"Teacher, we have something we want you to do for us."*
>
> *"What is it? I'll see what I can do."*
>
> *"Arrange it," they said, "so that we will be awarded the highest places of honor in your glory—one of us at your right, the other at your left."* [2]

James and John are called "the sons of thunder" and the moniker fits their stormy personalities. Whenever there is any type of resistance to Jesus' ministry, their suggested solution is to call down fire from heaven and incinerate those who get in the way. Like bolts of lightning, they strike first and hear the rumbles later.

Earlier, the disciples had argued among themselves about who was the greatest. At that time there was no resolution, just a firm rebuke from Jesus.

> *"So you want first place? Then take the last place. Be the servant of all."* [3]

Though reprimanded, James and John still push for the first place. The "sons of thunder" pull Jesus aside in order to push the other disciples out.

> *"Jesus, give us the highest places of honor—one at your right, the other at your left."*

Where there's lightning, rumbling soon follows. The brother's preemptive and presumptuous request sires a tempest among the other disciples. Tempers flare. Words fly. Accusations swirl.

> *When the other ten heard of this conversation, they lost their tempers with James and John. Jesus got them together to settle things down. "You've observed how godless rulers throw their weight around," he said, "and when people get a little power how quickly it goes to their heads. It's not going to be that way with you."* [4]

Jesus enters into the tumult. He grabs the disciples by their arms, separates them, sits them down, and tells them to cool off. When the red of rage has left their faces, Jesus begins once again to explain that life in the kingdom of God is a paradox: what's last is first; what's weak is strong; the one who serves is the one who rules.

Once more, he tries to explain that the cross inverts the values of the world—upside down to right side up. In the kingdom of God self-sacrifice sits on right side of the Messianic throne and servanthood on the left. These are the seats of honor.

*"Whoever wants to be great must become a servant.
Whoever wants to be first among you must be your slave.
That is what the Son of Man has done: He came to serve,
not to be served—and then to give away his life in
exchange for many who are held hostage."* [5]

As Jesus walks toward Jerusalem, he's preparing to die. Though the Jews will hand him over to Rome and Pilate will sentence him to death, they won't be the ones who will take his life. In fact, no one is going to steal Jesus' life; he's going to give it away.

He will voluntarily pay the ransom and become the sacrifice of substitution. Sin's hostages will be redeemed. Death's prisoners will be released. Heaven's children will be bought back, purchased by the Son. And from his cross, Jesus, the Messianic King, will rule. As he opens his arms to the nails, he'll give the gift of salvation: forgiveness of sins that sets the sinner free to serve.

Reflection

When was the last time you were in an argument or lost your temper with another Christ follower? What was it about?

Is there anything about the cross of Christ that you find hard to believe, abhorrent to think about, or loathsome to embrace?

How is Christ asking you to take the last place instead of the first? *We must become a servant as Christ lived a selfless life.*
What is your view of the kingdom of God and your place in it?

Prayer

Father,

Though your Son was the greatest, he became the least. He took on human flesh and set aside the privileges of deity. He became a servant—humble, lowly, and obedient. He lived a selfless life and died a sacrificial death. In life and in death, he gave his life away.

During this day, remind me of the price of redemption—the blood ransom—that was paid by Christ on the cross. When I am tempted to power up in my relationships, empower me to power down. When I scheme ways to sit at the highest places of honor, reverse my plans and make me available to serve in the low places—quietly, selflessly, and faithfully. When ambition nudges me to nudge others out, let me be the one to step aside. Help me spurn the lure of thrones and crowns and impassion me to embrace the paradox of the cross. Set me free to serve. In the Servant King's name I pray.

Amen

[1]Mark 10:32-34 [2]Mark 10:35-37 [3]Mark 9:35 [4]Mark 10:41-43 [5]Mark 10:43-45

He Knows My Reluctance To Love

Scripture Reading: Luke 10:25-42

Meditation

Jesus knows that love is an art and that the art of love is to take notice.

Ever since his ministry began, Jesus has been trying to paint pictures of what life is like in the kingdom of God. As he paints, the strokes of his brush are vigorous and his colors are vibrant, full of life. His images are vivid. His canvas is broad—love for the neighbor as well as for the Messiah. When once asked about the greatest commandment in the kingdom of God, he replied,

> " 'Love the Lord your God with all your passion and prayer
> and intelligence.' This is the most important, the first on
> any list. But there is a second to set alongside it: 'Love
> others as well as you love yourself.' These two commands
> are pegs; everything in God's Law and the Prophets
> hangs from them." [1]

But living such a life of love is often inconvenient. The troubles of others invade at inopportune times. A life of love is costly. It requires unexpected expenditures: money, energy, and emotion. Loving others as well as one loves self is counter-intuitive. For sinners, inwardly bent toward their own needs, it's unnatural to place the needs of the other over the wants of the self.

Though it is well received when given, such love is difficult to deliver. And so those who listen to Jesus begin to look for loopholes in the law of love. They want reasonable limits. Quotas. Narrowed definitions of "neighbor"—love "him", "her", but not "them."

A religion scholar stands up in the crowd and challenges Jesus,

> *"Teacher, what do I need to do to get eternal life?"* [2]

Jesus answers,

> *"What's written in God's Law? How do you interpret it?"*
>
> *He said, "That you love the Lord your God with all your passion and prayer and muscle and intelligence—and that you love your neighbor as well as you do yourself."*
>
> *"Good answer!" said Jesus. "Do it and you'll live."*
>
> *Looking for a loophole, he asked, "And just how would you define 'neighbor'?"* [3]

Jesus responds with a story.

A man on his way from Jerusalem to Jericho is robbed, beaten, and left for dead. Two religious men, a priest and a Levite, come upon the man but they fail to stop, refuse to help, and pass by on the other side. But a Samaritan—a mixed blood, and outcast, one hated and scorned by the Jews—when he sees the man in the ditch his heart goes out to him. He stops, cares for the man, takes him to an inn, and nurses him back to health.

After the story, Jesus asks the religion scholar,

> *"What do you think? Which of the three became a neighbor to the man attacked by robbers?"*
>
> *"The one who treated him kindly," the religion scholar responded.*
>
> *Jesus said, "Go and do the same."* [4]

Love—true love—notices.

This type of love stands at attention. Its eyes are fixed, posture is strong, ears are perked, and heart is seized by the needs of another. No distractions. No competition. There is only undivided attention—focused devotion and concentrated passion. All of one for the all of another: full passion, prayer, muscle, and intelligence fixed on the neighbor. These are the marks of true love.

As Jesus and his disciples continue to travel, he enters the village of Bethany. A woman named Martha opens her home to him and begins to prepare a banquet. But while she is working in the kitchen, her sister Mary sits at Jesus' feet, hanging on his every word. Martha, frazzled by her own busyness and frustrated by her sister's perceived idleness, interrupts Jesus.

> *"Master, don't you care that my sister has abandoned the kitchen to me? Tell her to lend me a hand."*
>
> *The Master said, "Martha, dear Martha, you're fussing far too much and getting yourself worked up over nothing. One thing only is essential, and Mary has chosen it—it's the main course, and won't be taken from her."* [5]

Martha's spirituality is trying to multitask. But in her activity, she supplants intimacy with the Savior. Doing for her Master replaces being with her Master. And eventually, her service crowds out affection.

Dirty dishes, casseroles, and table settings have taken precedence over Christ, the guest. Jesus tenderly admonishes her. He tells her that the moment busyness dominates; it slows the beat of love until intimacy lies cold in the heart.

The nature of Martha's world is that the petty yells and grabs center stage while that which is most precious waits patiently and whispers in the wings. Whether it's the Master sitting in the front room or a man lying in the ditch, that which is most needed is that which is most neglected.

In the kitchen or in the ditch along a dangerous road, that which is loved is that which is noticed.

Reflection

How is Christ calling you to love him with all your passion, prayer, muscle, and intelligence? How is he calling you to love your neighbor just as you would yourself?

What is the one essential thing in your life—the one thing needed? *love of my Lord*

How are you pulled away from the feet of Christ?
busyness.
Is your life full of activity for Christ or intimacy with him? How can you stop and sit at the Master's feet, hanging on his every word?

Prayer

Father,

In my life, love often takes the long way around. I often pass by on the other side, failing to slow myself or to take notice. When it comes to love, detours and distractions abound. All too many times, my activity gets in the way of intimacy. Your Son has so much to say and yet I am too busy to listen. Yet he doesn't yell. He waits patiently for the activity to calm and the noise to quiet. He desires whole body listening—passion, prayer, muscle, and intelligence.

During this day, make Christ the center of my attention. When I fuss too much or get worked up over nothing, pull me aside. Slow me down. Turn my gaze to the only essential thing—your Son. Remind me that dirty dishes can wait but Christ cannot. Help me sit at his feet, hanging on his every word, and in this way may I be captured by his love. It's in the name of Christ that I pray.

Amen.

[1]Matthew 22:37-40 [2]Luke 10:25 [3]Luke 10:26-29 [4]Luke 10:36-37
[5]Luke 10:40-42

Day 15:
He Knows My Rebellion

Scripture Reading: Matthew 16:13-28

Meditation

As Jesus walks toward Jerusalem, Israel's nationalistic morale is low but its Messianic expectations are high.

The crowd that follows this itinerant preacher from Nazareth is looking for someone to reclaim the crown of the kingdom of David. If Jesus wants to lead the rebellion against Rome, they're more than ready to follow. All he needs to do is give the word. But intermixed with the expectations are questions.

"Who is this Jesus? Where's he going?
What's he going to do when he gets there?"

Opinions are many. Answers are few.

Some say Jesus is John the Baptist, raised from the dead. Other's say he's Elijah, Jeremiah, or one of the other prophets. Still others hold their breath and dare to dream: he's the Christ, the promised Seed, the long-awaited and much-antici-pated royal Son of David. Most of the walking dialogue is casual; but occasionally, some of it turns into a heated debate.

As theories about Jesus swirl through the crowd, he presses his disciples for their opinion. He wants to know where they stand and how far they're willing to walk as they follow. Peter, the most assertive of the disciples, blurts out,

"You're the Christ, the Messiah, the Son of the living
God." [1]

Peter's confession is as solid as his nickname—"Rock." His convictions have always been firm and his passion resolute. But now his faith goes public. He goes on the record; Jesus is the Messiah and, where the Messiah goes, he will follow.

But when Jesus begins to explain to his disciples that he must go to Jerusalem and walk the way of the cross, it's Peter who rebels.

> *Then Jesus made it clear to his disciples that it was now necessary for him to go to Jerusalem, submit to an ordeal of suffering at the hands of the religious leaders, be killed, and then on the third day be raised up alive. Peter took him in hand, protesting, "Impossible, Master! That can never be!"* [2]

Peter's iron will sharpens steel words against his Master. His rebuke is sharp. He jumps in front of Jesus and blocks his path to the cross. Though Jesus tries to move around him, Peter shadow steps him, all the while protesting his Master's plans to his face.

> *"No way, Master!*
> *You've got it all wrong! I won't let it happen!"*

Peter leaves no room for dialogue. His rebuke is more than resistance; it's open rebellion, a public revolt. When Peter hears his Master talking about the suffering that awaits the Messiah in Jerusalem, every rock-like conviction in him begins to roll down hill. An avalanche of passion begins to gather. Out of control, Peter, tries to sweep Jesus away with the force of his emotions. He forgets who's the Master and who's the disciple.

The same Peter who minutes earlier publicly confessed that Jesus was the Messiah, the very Son of God, now jumps in and takes the lead away from his Master. The rock and cornerstone of Christ's church has just become a stumbling block. He refuses allegiance to Jesus and resists his authority. He stiff-arms the Son of God. His rebellion is a claim that he knows more than his Master does. Peter demands that Jesus follow him. He believes that his way is better—it leads to a crown and not the cross.

As Peter's emotions tumble downhill, Jesus stands still. He doesn't jump out of the way. He takes the full force of Peter's words. Standing still, he listens, but only for a moment. As soon as Peter pauses to take a breath, Jesus jumps into the tirade and identifies the real voice behind Peter's upbraiding.

> *"Peter, get out of my way. Satan, get lost. You have no idea how God works."* [3]

Peter may be the obstacle but Jesus sees someone else as the source of the obstruction. He identifies the real rebel—Satan.

But no uprising, from disciples or demons, will stop Jesus from going the way of the cross. He is determined to take the road less traveled. He takes a step forward, and this time, Peter steps out of the way. The Master retakes the lead. He begins again to walk toward the cross. Where he leads, he asks his disciples to follow.

"Anyone who intends to come with me has to let me lead. You're not in the driver's seat; I am. Don't run from suffering; embrace it. Follow me and I'll show you how. Self-help is no help at all. Self-sacrifice is the way, my way, to finding yourself, your true self. What kind of deal is it to get everything you want but lose yourself? What could you ever trade your soul for?" [4]

As Jesus explains the way of the cross, his words are clear. Though the cross leads to death, the path of suffering won't lead to a dead end. On the third day he will rise again. And whoever follows him into the grave will walk out of the tomb. After the cross, comes the resurrection.

Reflection

In what ways have you become a stumbling block to Christ?

Who do you say that Christ is? What is his work?

In what areas of your life are you saying, *"Impossible, Master! That can never be!"*

In what way is Christ asking you to get out of the "driver's seat" and let him lead?

Prayer

Father,

Where your Son leads, he asks me to follow. But the road that he walks is the way of the cross and the cross is a painful place to go. His is a path that leads to death, loss, and sacrifice—destinations unwanted and unwelcome. Many times I have stepped in front of your Son. I've stood my ground and rebuked him to his face. I have resisted his ways,

"Impossible, Master! That can never be!"

During this day, remind me that though your Son said that he must go the cross, he also said that, after his crucifixion—on the third day—he would rise again. Assure me that if I am united with Christ in his death, that I will also be united with him in his resurrection.

When your Son calls me to follow, put to death my rebellion. Breathe new life into me and then resurrect in me a surrendered life. Push Satan out of the path that leads to the cross. Clear any and all obstacles that impede the way of Christ in my life. Assure me that he will walk with me into the grave and out of the tomb. In all things may the Messiah take the lead. It's in his name that I pray.

Amen.

[1]Matthew 16:16 [2]Matthew 16:21-22 [3]Matthew 16:23 [4]Matthew 16:24-26

Day 16:

He Knows My Refusal To Forgive

Scripture Reading: Matthew 18:15-35

Meditation

Peter's been hurt one too many times. One of his fellow believers has taken advantage of the gift of grace and has turned it into a license: a sanction to sin. To Peter's credit, he's tried to work it out. Step by step, he's followed the law of love: in all things try and win the brother.

> "If a fellow believer hurts you, go and tell him — work it out between the two of you. If he listens, you've made a friend. If he won't listen, take one or two others along so that the presence of witnesses will keep things honest, and try again. If he still won't listen, tell the church. If he won't listen to the church, you'll have to start over from scratch, confront him with the need for repentance, and offer again God's forgiving love." [1]

Peter's been generous in his forgiveness. Seven times he's erased the man's debt, four more times than that suggested by the rabbis. But this unruly brother is like a dog returning to his vomit; whatever sin he swallows in feigned repentance, he keeps throwing up.

When confronted, he's quick to accept Peter's gift of forgiveness. He unwraps, opens it, and even says, "Thank you." But then, as soon as Peter's back is turned, this brother takes the gift of grace, rewraps it, and returns it with a dagger hidden inside.

For Peter, it's the same painful stab, with the same knife, in the same place; it's just done on a different day. Wounded, Peter wonders,

"When is enough, enough?"

As Jesus talks about the economy of forgiveness in the kingdom of God, Peter begins to do the math: How much is too much? How often is too often? What's the limit point? Where's the line in the sand? Finally, Peter gets up the nerve to ask Jesus,

"Master, how many times do I forgive a brother or sister who hurts me? Seven?" [2]

In response to his own question, Peter offers up a generous response—seven times, more than double the amount required by rabbinical law. But Jesus stops the calculations. He tells Peter to put the ledger away. No more talk of debits and credits. The kingdom of God isn't about balancing the books between brothers; it's about infinite grace for immeasurable offense.

Jesus responds,

"Seven! Hardly. Try seventy times seven." [3]

Seventy times seven. Jesus makes it clear that, in his kingdom, forgiveness isn't a measurable entity. It can't be portioned out like a month's worth of staples or rationed like water in a desert. In the kingdom of God, there are no limits. The King has no quotas. Earthly forgiveness has no ceiling because heaven's grace has no roof. In the economy of the kingdom, if forgiveness between brothers is the currency, then the grace of God is the gold standard that backs it up.

For Peter, the math is still fuzzy and so Jesus tells him a story in order to illustrate the economics of the kingdom of God.

> *"The kingdom of God is like a king who decided to square accounts with his servants. As he got under way, one servant was brought before him who had run up a debt of a hundred thousand dollars. He couldn't pay up, so the king ordered the man, along with his wife, children, and goods, to be auctioned off at the slave market."*

> *"The poor wretch threw himself at the king's feet and begged, 'Give me a chance and I'll pay it all back.' Touched by his plea, the king let him off, erasing the debt."* [4]

Jesus goes on to relate that, no sooner did the servant leave the presence of the king than he came upon a fellow servant who owed him ten dollars. The forgiven servant seized the man by his throat and demanded payment. Though the man begged for mercy, the servant took no pity on him and had him thrown into debtor's prison. Those who stood watching were outraged and ran to the king and told him everything that had happened. The king was furious and sent for the man. As the servant stood cowering before the king, the king reopened the man's account, reapplied the one hundred thousand dollar debt, threw the man into debtor's prison, and had the screws put to him until he paid the amount in full.

Jesus ends the story by saying,

> *"And that's exactly what my Father in heaven is going to do to each one of you who doesn't forgive unconditionally anyone who asks for mercy."* [5]

These are strong words for strong wills. They are filled with fiery force because failure to forgive the brother is an affront to the grace of the King. When Jesus asks Peter to forgive, he's only asking him to do what he himself has already done—given infinite grace for immeasurable offense.

In the King's kingdom, forgiveness knows no limits. Jesus doesn't excuse the sin but he does pardon the sinner. In an act of sacrifice, he absorbs the loss and pays off the balance himself. In his kingdom, there will be no debts. No debtors. Sin is forgiven. Grace is received. Mercy, in abundance, is to be given to others.

"Keep us forgiven with you and forgiving others." [6]

This is the prayer of the kingdom.

Reflection

In what way are you begging for forgiveness? How much do you owe the King?

Who owes you? Are you willing to cancel such debts?

Why is it so easy to receive forgiveness and so hard to forgive?

Are there any limits to your forgiveness? Do you struggle with "how much" or "how often?"

Prayer

Father,

Forgiveness is so easy to receive but so hard to give. I beg for it for myself, but, when it's lavished upon me, I begrudge it to others. Though your forgiveness has no limits, I limit it. I never tire of receiving it but when I'm asked to give it away to a brother or sister who has hurt me, I wonder, "How much more? How often? When is enough, enough?"

During this day, overwhelm me with the bounty of your love and then let me forgive out of that abundance. Help me see that I always owe you more than what my brother or sister owes me. As forgiveness was the defining mark of my Savior's life, may it also define the way that I live. When I hesitate to give mercy, remind me that immeasurable grace has been poured over my innumerable offenses. Keep me forgiven and forgiving others. It's in your Son's name that I pray.

Amen.

---

[1]Matthew 18:15-17 [2]Matthew 18:21 [3]Matthew 18:22 [4]Matthew 18:23-27
[5]Matthew 18:35 [6]Matthew 6:12

The Shelter of Rest

"True to your word, you let me catch my breath, and send me in the right direction."

Psalm 23:3

Every journey has its share of starts and stops and it's only the better part of wisdom that knows when it's time to do which. Though the Good Shepherd asks his sheep to follow, he never outruns the flock. His pace might be steady but his steps never stride beyond the cries of the smallest lamb. Though some straggle, none are left behind. The Shepherd is always attentive to the needs of his flock.

> He knows when they need to stop.
> He knows how long the sheep need to catch
>   their breath.
> He knows when to rouse the sheep and in what
>   direction they need to start again.

As you rest awhile during these forty days with Christ, reflect on the following ...

Reflection

When was the last time you felt like you were out of spiritual breath?

How has the Good Shepherd been true to his word and given you rest? *Through study of His word - 40 days with the good Shepherd —*

In what way is he leading you in the right direction?

Day 17:
He Knows My Shame

Scripture Reading: John 8:1-11

Meditation

She's a woman who's looking for Mr. Right in the wrong bed.

It's dawn. As the rest of the women in the village are getting dressed and going out the front door to do the morning chores, she's sneaking through the back door of her neighbor's house, getting undressed, taking off her wedding ring, and sliding under the covers into her lover's embrace.

The forbidden embrace feels all so right. And because it feels all so right, she wonders why it's said to be all so wrong. Even if it is wrong, no one knows about it. Neither spouse suspects. Friends don't have a clue. And as long as they keep the affair under the covers, no one will get hurt. After all, secret sins bring with them no public shame.

But on this morning, the secret affair is about to become public knowledge. The lovers aren't the only ones sneaking around in the shadows. In the closet, Pharisaical peeping eyes are watching. Somehow the religious leaders have found out about the affair.

Unbeknownst to the woman, her lover has decided to cut a deal with the religion scholars: his skin for her neck. For dubious reasons, the religious leaders need to catch the woman in the act of adultery.

In exchange for her lover's cooperation, they agree that, when the time comes, they'll let him sneak out the back door a free man but they'll drag her into the temple courts to stand before Jesus.

As the woman slips into her lover's bed, the religious leaders watch. They wait. When they've seen enough of her sin to make their case, they jump out of their hiding place and pull the woman out of the bed. They push her, half clothed, through the streets toward the temple courts, and bring her before Jesus.

> *The religion scholars and Pharisees led in a woman who had been caught in an act of adultery. They stood her in plain sight of everyone and said, "Teacher, this woman was caught red-handed in the act of adultery. Moses, in the Law, gives orders to stone such persons. What do you say?" They were trying to trap him into saying something incriminating so they could bring charges against him.* [1]

She's been caught in the act. No hearsay. No suspicion. There are eyewitnesses. The same religious leaders who witnessed her sin in private are the ones who now put her sin on public display. As she stands before Jesus, she's physically and spiritually exposed. She feels more than guilt; she feels shame. Guilt exposes her actions. Shame exposes her. With such shame come the taunts from the crowd:

"Home wrecker.
  Adulteress. Whore."

The Pharisees and the religion scholars don't care about her. Truth be told, they're not even concerned about her act of adultery because hidden beneath their condemnation is a hook. She's only the bait for their trap; Jesus is the real prize. Her sin is just the scent they need to lure Jesus out into the open. When he opens his mouth, they're hoping that he'll say something incriminating. Then they'll have something substantial to charge him with.

The religious leaders put her in the middle of the temple courts. As they encircle her with a ring of judgment, they throw questions toward Jesus.

> *"What do you say, Jesus?*
> *Keep the Law or save the woman?*
> *Come on now! Which will it be?"*

Their questions pose a spiritual dilemma. Either Jesus has to swing the hammer of justice or extend the hand of grace. They're hoping that their questions will force him to choose between the Law of Moses and his love for sinners. They know that Jesus can't have it both ways. Like the promoters of a dog-fight, they're pitting condemnation and compassion. When Jesus picks one, he will kill the other. Either way, the religious leaders will be there to collect the winnings.

As the woman's accusers badger Jesus for an answer, he bends down and scratches something in the ground. The Pharisees and religion scholars are more than willing to play the parts of plaintiff, judge, and jury. When they begin to pick up the stones and raise their hands to play the role of executioner, however, Jesus questions their qualifications. After a prolonged silence, he stands up and gives his answer. It's direct and, in its directness, it presents the religious leaders with their own dilemma.

> *"The sinless one among you, go first: Throw the stone."* [2]

Only the sinless are invited to throw stones. Beginning with the oldest, the religious leaders lower their hands, drop their stones, walk away from the woman, and leave the circle of judgment. No one is innocent. No one is left except Jesus.

Hearing that, they walked away, one after another,
beginning with the oldest. The woman was left alone.
Jesus stood up and spoke to her. "Woman, where are they?
Does no one condemn you?"

"No one, Master."

"Neither do I," said Jesus. "Go on your way. From now on,
don't sin." [3]

Her Messiah is the only one qualified to condemn her and
yet he holds no stones. Instead, as he speaks to her, he
removes the scarlet robe of her shame and covers her with his
grace. He forgives her and tells her to go on her way. But as
she leaves, he tells her to stop her old way of living and invites
her to a new life. Where sin is forgiven, there is no longer
any shame.

Reflection

What does it feel like to get caught in the act of your sin and have it exposed to all of those around you?

Are you holding any stones? Who are you ready to throw them at?

Jesus said to the woman caught in adultery, *"Go on your way. From now on, don't sin."*

What way of life is Jesus asking you to stop?

What life is he inviting you to begin?

Prayer

Father,

I have looked for love in all the wrong places. All too many times you have caught me in the act of my sin. You see the adultery. You know about the betrayal. You've exposed my love affair with the things of this world and laid bare my infidelity. I am full of shame and deserve to stand in the center of the circle of judgment and have rocks of condemnation thrown at me.

During this day, show me once again that your Son stands in the circle of judgment next to me. When others condemn me, he shields me. His grace doesn't excuse my sin. He doesn't justify it but he does forgive it. Remind me that, when he tells me to leave my old life, he's inviting me to begin anew. Forgiven, may I no longer live in shame. It's in Jesus' name that I pray.

Amen.

¹John 8:3-6 ²John 8:7 ³John 8:9-11

Day 18:

He Knows My Determination

Scripture Reading: Mark 7:24-30

Meditation

On the northwest border of Galilee, in the region of Phoenicia, are the cities of Tyre and Sidon—ancient homes to the pagan fertility cults of Baal and Ashtoreth. According to the oral law, Jews were not to have any association with these Gentiles. Anyone who broke with the law and had contact with the filthy dogs from the north would be declared ritually unclean.

Jesus breaks with the tradition of the elders and makes a break for Tyre. He leaves Galilee, disregards the ceremonial injunction, and deliberately heads for the "polluted regions" of the north. He is bone tired, ministry weary, and still grieving the execution of his friend and forerunner, John the Baptist. As he nears the city, he looks for a hideaway, a secret place where he can rest and pray.

> *He entered a house there where he didn't think he would be found, but he couldn't escape notice.* [1]

Tyre was supposed to be a place of anonymity for Jesus: a place where nobody knew his name and therefore, no one would want anything from him. But no matter where Jesus goes, people follow. The needy search him out. The desperate get creative and find ways to get to him. Those who hurt are determined to find help and they don't stop until they are heard.

Pain gives them perseverance.

> *He was barely inside when a woman who had a disturbed daughter heard where he was. She came and knelt at his feet, begging for help. The woman was Greek, Syro-Phoenician by birth. She asked him to cure her daughter.* [2]

The woman is a Gentile. Born a Syro-Phoenician, she's a daughter of Israel's ancient enemies. But today she waves no nationalistic flag. She marches under no banner. She carries no sign touting her political or cultural agenda. The only badge that she wears is that of "mother" and her only cause is the release of her demon-possessed daughter.

Living with her daughter is like living with a rabid dog. When the demon grabs hold of her baby girl, her daughter foams at the mouth, bares her teeth, and growls. Day after day, the tormenter assaults her child. There is no rest for her daughter or respite for her.

When the demon first came, the mother was overcome by fear but now maternal instincts drive her. She's angry—attack the child and you attack the mother. She will not let her daughter suffer any longer. Somewhere there has to be someone who can do something for her daughter.

One of her friends had told her about Jesus. Rumor had it that he was a miracle worker from Galilee and that he was making his way into the neighborhood. That's all that this mother needed to hear.

Like a bloodhound fresh on the scent, she tracked Jesus down and cornered him just inside the door of his hideaway. But now, gentle as a lapdog, she lays at his feet and whimpers for grace. She's not beyond getting down on all fours and pleading for mercy. Her daughter is more important than her pride.

Her begging is met with a gruff response from Jesus,

"Stand in line and take your turn. The children get fed first. If there's any left over, the dogs get it." 3

Jesus tells her to get to the back of the line. There seems to be a pecking order in the Messianic ministry of Jesus. The privileged children of Israel get to eat from the gospel table first and then, if there's anything left, the Gentile dogs under the table are welcome to the scraps. But while the children are eating, the dogs have to wait. There are no cuts in line.

The mother doesn't challenge Jesus' answer. She doesn't argue for an exception to the rule of precedence or howl on about her rights. She doesn't bark out any complaint. She admits her 'under the table' status but refuses to believe that she is to be excluded from any of the benefits of the kingdom of God, even if they are the leftovers. She simply agrees with Jesus and once more whimpers for help.

"Of course, Master. But don't dogs under the table get scraps dropped by the children?" 4

Her reply is a crumb of truth that contains a loaf of wisdom. Jesus is impressed.

"You're right! On your way! Your daughter is no longer disturbed. The demonic affliction is gone." She went home and found her daughter relaxed on the bed, the torment gone for good. 5

Jesus throws this mother more than a bone; he pulls up a chair, invites her to sit at the table, and throws her a feast. No more torment. No more terror. The black dog of despair is gone for good.

With this miracle, the bounty of the Messianic kingdom is no longer limited to the privileged children of Israel. There is no longer any preferred seating. The table is open to all who are hungry for a scrap of mercy and hope for a morsel of grace.

Reflection

What torment are you experiencing? What scrap of mercy are you begging for?

When you pray, what or who do you fight for?

Which do you feel like when you pray?

The privileged child who is sitting at the banquet table?

Or one of the dogs that is waiting for the scraps?

Prayer

Father,

Many times I feel like a dog begging under the table of your bounty. Others seem to get preferred seating while I have to settle for the crumbs. There are many hunger pains in my life: tormenting illness, slanted circumstances, fractured relationships, stillborn dreams, frustrated desires. But the pain brings with it persistence—a dogged determination to crawl to your feet and beg for a morsel of mercy.

During this day, remind me that, in Christ, there is no preferred seating at the table of grace. All are welcome. There are no leftovers. Like the mother with the tormented daughter, may I come to your Son with tenacity and no regard for pride, determined to whimper my request before the feet of my Savior. In grace, may he encourage me to go on my way. No more torment. No more terror. If it is your will, let the thing that dogs me be gone for good. It's in Jesus' name that I pray.

Amen.

[1]Mark 7:24 [2]Mark 7:25-26 [3]Mark 7:27 [4]Mark 7:28 [5]Mark 7:29-30

Day 19:
He Knows My Hunger

Scripture Reading: John 6:22-59

Meditation

Less than twenty-four hours ago, Jesus had taken a little boy's lunch, looked toward heaven, blessed the five barley loaves and two fishes, multiplied them, and threw a kingdom picnic for more than five thousand growling stomachs. Those gathered on the grassy hill ate as much as they wanted. They stuffed themselves to the full. And when they had finished eating, there were twelve baskets overflowing with leftovers. Jesus, just like Moses, had delivered bread from heaven. When the people saw this miraculous sign they began to wonder if Jesus could be the Messiah.

Talk around the picnic blanket centered on the possibility of Jesus being the long awaited Prophet, the Anointed One who was promised to come out from among his own people. With bellies full and guts empty of any worries, the table talk moved from conversation to consensus: Jesus just might be the next Moses—provider, deliverer, miracle worker, and leader of a new exodus.

"This is the Prophet for sure, God's Prophet right here in Galilee!" [1]

As the sun began to set, talk turned to action. Driven by the satisfaction in their stomachs, the crowd coalesced and marched up the hillside set on crowning Jesus as their king. But before the crowd could reach him, Jesus slipped away and escaped to a secluded place up the mountain.

115

Reaching a quiet place, Jesus begins to pray. As he prays, his Father reminds him of his temptation in the wilderness, the forty-day fast. At the end of the forty days, he was more than hungry; he was famished. That was his weakest and most vulnerable moment and, in that moment, Satan suggested that he turn stones into loaves of bread. But as the fangs of famine bit into his gut, the bread of Scripture sustained his soul. Jesus rebuked the suggestion of the Serpent,

> *"It takes more than bread to stay alive. It takes a steady stream of words from God's mouth."* [2]

In the wilderness, Jesus had shunned the coronation of a physical kingdom by the Evil One and now, on the mount in Galilee, he does the same. He is a king but not the type of king that the crowd is looking for. They want a king that is constantly cooking in heaven's kitchen—a Messiah who rules the mess hall. They're dreaming of a Christ who will provide unlimited food and drink, anytime, anywhere, prepared any way they want it.

But Jesus wants to give his followers more than bread; he wants to give life—lasting life. Bread from heaven might fill the stomach for a day but Jesus wants them, by faith, to sink their teeth into something more substantial: the Bread of Life that satisfies for an eternity.

The next day, as the crowd wakes up, their stomachs begin to growl and they go looking for Jesus. When they can't find him, they take some boats and set out for Capernaum, where his disciples had gone without him the night before. When they reach the other side of the lake, they find Jesus walking the shore and they wonder when he had arrived. Jesus sees the real craving behind their search.

"You've come looking for me not because you saw God in my actions but because I fed you, filled your stomachs—and for free."

"Don't waste your energy striving for perishable food like that. Work for the food that sticks with you, food that nourishes your lasting life, food the Son of Man provides. He and what he does are guaranteed by God the Father to last." [3]

A growling stomach, and not an ache in the soul, drives the crowd to look for Jesus. The masses are hungry and they're on the hunt. They want someone like Moses who morning by morning, will fill their stomachs, gratify their cravings, soothe their hunger pangs, and satisfy their appetites with a constant flow of manna.

Jesus sees beyond their growling stomachs. He sees the emptiness and the cravings that hold them captive. Yesterday, he had filled their stomachs. Today, he wants to fill their souls. More than barley bread that gets stale and grows mold, Jesus wants to offer himself.

"I am the Bread of Life. The person who aligns with me hungers no more and thirsts no more, ever." [4]

But before the people sink their teeth into Jesus, they want a sign. Popular opinion has it that the Messiah would be one who would be greater than Moses. He would lead another exodus and would, along the way, satisfy every physical craving. They compare Jesus to Moses.

"Jesus might have fed five thousand but Moses fed an entire nation. Jesus filled our stomachs one time; Moses did it for forty years. Jesus gives ordinary bread; Moses gave 'bread from heaven.'"

Jesus responds,

> *"I'm telling you the most solemn and sober truth now:*
> *Whoever believes in me has real life, eternal life. I am the*
> *Bread of Life. Your ancestors ate the manna bread in the*
> *desert and died. But now here is Bread that truly comes*
> *down out of heaven. Anyone eating this Bread will not*
> *die, ever. I am the Bread—living Bread!—who came down*
> *out of heaven. Anyone who eats this Bread will live—and*
> *forever! The Bread that I present to the world so that it*
> *can eat and live is myself, this flesh-and-blood self."* [5]

The proof is in the eating. Manna may satisfy for a day but the Messiah satisfies for a lifetime.

Reflection

What does it mean to have a full stomach but an empty soul? Which do you have?

What is the recurrent hunger in your life? How is Christ using that hunger to draw you to him?

How is the Bread of Life nourishing your soul?

When Jesus says, *"It takes more than bread to stay alive. It takes a steady stream of words from God's mouth." (Matthew 4:4),* what does that mean?

Prayer

Father,

Many times I have run after your Son looking for food for my stomach rather than nourishment for my soul. I see Jesus as a bread king and not the Messiah—a cook in the kitchen and not the Savior on the cross. All too many times, in all the wrong ways, I crave that which sustains the body but cannot sustain the soul.

During this day, give me faith so that I might have a belief that bites into the reality of Christ. Though it's hard for me to understand, help me feed on your Son's flesh and blood. May I sink my teeth into the words that come from his mouth so that I might swallow, in faith, the promise of the Bread of Life. As I swallow, may Christ live in me in a mysterious way. Show me today that manna satisfies for a day but the Messiah satisfies for a lifetime. It's in his name that I pray.

Amen.

---

[1]John 6:14   [2]Matthew 4:4   [3]John 6:26-27   [4]John 6:35   [5]John 6:47-51

Day 20:
He Knows My Darkness

Scripture Reading: John 9:1-41

Meditation

Ever since his ministry began, Jesus has been invading the dark places.

When Nicodemus came to him in the middle of the night, Jesus struck a match of love to guide him on his way. As Jesus sat by the well in Sychar, he kindled acceptance around a five time divorced Samaritan woman who was hiding in her shame. When asked to pass judgment on a woman who was caught in the act of adultery, he stoked the fires of forgiveness.

Wherever he went, Jesus blazed like the sun.

His love brought warmth, his words illumination.

> *"I am the world's Light. No one who follows me stumbles around in the darkness. I provide plenty of light to live in."* [1]

One day, as Jesus left the temple grounds, he saw a beggar sitting by the side of the road, a man blind from birth. All the beggar knows, and has ever known, is darkness.

No sunrises or sunsets.
No color, except the ink black of his days and nights.
No faces or expressions, only voices.

Though his eyes are sealed shut, his ears are always open. When he's near the temple grounds, he overhears people talking with the rabbis about his plight. They wonder why he was born blind.

The rabbis explain the man's darkness by quoting the words of the Law.

> *"Still, he (God) doesn't ignore sin. He holds sons and grandsons responsible for a father's sins to the third and even fourth generation."* [2]

It's a tidy explanation for a messy situation.

For the religious authorities, the man's blindness is both theological and logical. After all, infirmities like this just don't randomly happen. There has to be a cause for every effect.

Somewhere in the man's past, there was wrongdoing. His blindness had to be the just result of a sin; the sin produced a curse and the curse was passed down from generation to generation.

The rabbis are fond of quoting,

> *"There is no death without sin,*
> *and there is no suffering without iniquity."*

As the disciples pass by the blind man, they ask Jesus some of the same questions. They want to know the root cause of the blind man's condition. They don't ask out of compassion but out of curiosity.

They see the man more as a theological riddle to be solved than someone who is riddled with pain. They want to know it all: who's to blame, why it happened, where it went wrong, all so that they can make sure it doesn't happen to them.

The disciples' minds are clouded. They're asking the wrong questions. Like the first rays of the sun cutting through the stormy darkness, Jesus shines a divine light on the man's life.

> *"You're asking the wrong question. You're looking for someone to blame. There is no such cause-effect here. Look instead for what God can do. We need to be energetically at work for the One who sent me here, working while the sun shines. When night falls, the workday is over. For as long as I am in the world, there is plenty of light. I am the world's Light."* [3]

The disciples want to know who's to blame but Jesus wants to show them what God can do.

According to Jesus ...

The man's darkness isn't a punishment.
It's not a generational curse.
It's an opportunity for the Messiah to do
his illuminating work.

Going over to the man, Jesus spits in the dust and makes a clay paste with the saliva. He puts it on the man's eyes and tells him to go the Pool of Siloam and wash.

Immediately, the man stumbles his way to the pool, washes the mud from his eyes, and for the first time, sees.

Light. Colors.
People. Places.

The miracle is so amazing that, when his neighbors see him running through the streets, they rub their eyes in disbelief. Some say that he's the blind man who used to sit and beg. Others say that it couldn't possibly be him; it must be his twin.

After further investigation, they all realize that it isn't a case of mistaken identity; he is the man who was born blind. Stunned, they march the man to the Pharisees to get an explanation.

Because the healing had occurred on the Sabbath, the Pharisees grill the man. After hearing his story about Jesus, they're split in their opinion.

Some hold to the Sabbath law and deny the validity of the miracle and the miracle worker. Others embrace the miracle and trace its origin back to the Messiah.

After all, the prophet Isaiah did say,

> *At that time the deaf will hear*
> *word-for-word what's been written.*
> *After a lifetime in the dark,*
> *the blind will see.* [4]

Embedded in the middle of the controversy is the man born blind.

The religious authorities tell him to give credit where credit is due. They reason that Jesus couldn't possibly be the Messiah because he broke the Sabbath. Whoever breaks the Sabbath, they believe, is a sinner; furthermore, everyone knows that God doesn't listen to sinners. So this Jesus has to be an impostor.

To which the man simply replies,

"I know nothing about that one way or the other. But I know one thing for sure: I was blind ... I now see." [5]

Though the Messiah is blazing in their presence, the only one who can see the Light of the World is the one who had been in the dark.

Unwilling to validate the work of the miracle worker, the Pharisees degrade the man in front of his friends, excommunicate him from the family of the synagogue, ostracize him from society, and throw him back out into the darkness of the streets.

When Jesus hears that the religious authorities have thrown the man out of the synagogue, he goes on a search for the man.

Finding him he asks,

"Do you believe in the Son of Man?"

The man said, "Point him out to me, sir, so that I can believe in him."

Jesus said, "You're looking right at him. Don't you recognize my voice?"

"Master, I believe," the man said, and worshiped him. [6]

As soon as the man matches the loving tone of his healer's voice to the tender look on Jesus' face, he falls at his feet and worships him.

The Light of the World does his best work in the darkest places.

 Verse 41 ??

Reflection

What dark places are there in your life?

How do you view the dark places in your life? Do you see them as punishments from God or opportunities for him to do his best work?

How has the Light of the World done his best work in your darkness?

What's your testimony? In what ways were you once blind but now you can see?

Prayer

Father,

There are many dark places in my life. Like the blind man who sat by the side of the road, I wonder if the darkness is a direct result of my sin or simply the ever-present reality of living in a broken and depraved world. Whatever the cause, remind me that your Son is the Light of the World. Assure me that he sees my darkness, not as a disqualification for grace, but as an opportunity to do his best work.

During this day, send your Light. Illuminate me. Enlighten me. Warm me. Open my eyes to see the face of Christ. When I can't see the face of Christ, help me listen for the cadence, pitch, and tender tone of his voice. When the darkness lifts and people see me running through the streets, and wonder what has happened to me, help me tell my salvation story— *"I once was blind ... now I see."* It's in Jesus' name that I pray.

Amen

[1]John 8:12 [2]Exodus 34:7 [3]John 9:3-5 [4]Isaiah 29:18 [5]John 9:25 [6]John 9:35-38

Day 21:
He Knows My Demons

Scripture Reading: Mark 5:1-20

Meditation

Across the Sea of Galilee, on the east side of the lake, is the Gentile region of Gerasene. Nestled close to the shore is a small village, central base for the pig herders in the area and former home to the man possessed by a legion of demons.

South of the village is a cliff with a steep slope that runs a straight slant directly into the lake. A few miles from the slope are the cavern tombs, limestone beds reserved for the sleep of the dead. And living among the dead is the village madman, the Gerasene demoniac.

He wasn't always deranged. Before he was overcome by the demons, he was a respectable young man in the community. Responsible. Trustworthy. Willing to work hard. He loved his family, had a way with the children in the village, and was soon planning to marry. His dreams were full of life and his life was full of hope.

But some time ago, as he was tending his father's pigs, he was ambushed by a mob of rioting demons. Two thousand of hell's henchmen jumped out of the shadows and assaulted him. The more he resisted, the more they fought. The more they fought, the weaker he became. Finally and fully, they possessed him.

The mob of demons now owns him. It has taken over every part of his life: speech, sleep, steps, moods, actions, emotions, dreams, and desires. Apart from the will and whims of the thugs that torment him, the man is unable to act. They have taken his life but have left him alive. He's become one of the living dead. No hope. No will. No freedom. He's a prisoner held captive in his own body. He's alive and yet he's dead. That's why he lives among the tombs.

Though the demon possessed man used to live among the villagers, his friends and family now fear him. He's become a danger to himself as well as to all of those in the area, especially the children.

Day and night they find him haunting the hills, screaming, slashing himself with rocks, harassing the herdsmen, raiding the pigs, and scaring the children. The elders of the village have tried to restrain him many times. But the demons that bind the madman are more powerful than the ropes and chains that the elders use. No one, nor any one thing, is strong enough to subdue him.

The elders finally give up. It isn't flesh and blood that they're fighting; it's something stronger, darker, and more sinister. It's the devil's grip that they're trying to loosen and only heaven can pry hell's fingers off of the man.

Until further notice, everyone in the village is warned to stay out of the madman's way. All they can do for him is hope for the best and pray that the worst doesn't happen.

One afternoon, as the madman rants through the hills, he sees a storm-weary boat approach the shore. Earlier that day, as he stood on the cliffs, he had watched the sky rear its head in rebellion. Thunder and lightning were throwing a tantrum in the heavens and, as the madman stood open-armed in the downpour, the demons reveled in the turbulence. Such violence and agitation; nature was mirroring the weather of the man's soul. But suddenly the rage stopped. Chaos went directly to calm. It was as if the tempest had been bound and gagged.

The boat that approaches the Gerasene shore had just rocked its way through the middle of that storm. In it are Jesus and his disciples. A few hours earlier, the winds had bullied the boat. They had blown the disciples across the lake to the brink of terror.

During it all, Jesus, their Master, was fast asleep in the stern, head on a pillow, body at rest. But after being shaken awake by his disciples, the Master stood up in the boat, rubbed the sleep from his eyes, raised his hands, spoke into the tempest, and shackled the storm.

> *"Quiet! Settle down!" The wind ran out of breath; the sea became smooth as glass.* [1]

When Jesus spoke, wind and sea obeyed. They shut their mouths, bowed their heads in reverence, and submitted to the rebuke of the Son of God. Nature knows the voice of authority.

Now, as Jesus sets foot on the Gerasene shore, it's time for the supernatural to surrender to the Messiah. The mob of demons charge toward Jesus and a war begins. The madman's body becomes the battlefield.

At first, the demons bow the man low in homage but then they begin to bellow in protest.

> *"What business do you have, Jesus, Son of the High God, messing with me? I swear to God, don't give me a hard time!" (Jesus had just commanded the tormenting evil spirit, "Out! Get out of the man!")* [2]

Realizing that one more powerful is in front of them and that the battle is futile, the mob of demons tries to cut a deal of exemption. Though unwilling to show any mercy to the man they possess, they beg for mercy for themselves.

"Send us to the pigs so we can live in them." Jesus gave the order. But it was even worse for the pigs than for the man. Crazed, they stampeded over a cliff into the sea and drowned. [3]

As suddenly as the demons had come, now they're gone. The demons, bent on the man's destruction, have been hogtied by the Messiah. Finally the man is free.

Having given the man his life back, Jesus also gives him a mission. He's to go home and tell his story.

"Go home to your own people. Tell them your story—what the Master did, how he had mercy on you." The man went back and began to preach in the Ten Towns area about what Jesus had done for him. He was the talk of the town. [4]

Reflection

Do you ever feel like one of the living dead? If so, what does it feel like?

What type of "rioting mob" torments you?

When you kneel before the Messiah, what parts of you bow in worship? What parts bellow in protest?

If Jesus were to tell you to go home and tell your family all that he had done for you, what would you say? What's your story?

Prayer

Father,

I see so many other people living—really living—while I rant and rage among the tombs, keeping company with the dead. There are many days when I feel like the man possessed by the mob of demons—ambushed by Satan's thugs, bound, gagged, and dragged away from my friends and family, harassed and tormented day and night by anxiety within and fears without, overcome by despair, locked firm in the Devil's grip, dead and yet very much alive.

During this day, send your Son to confront the demons that own me. Though the rioting mob may bellow in protest, when they see the Messiah may they bow before him in worship. Just as your Son freed the village madman, may he hogtie my demons. Give me a clear mind, a pure heart, a mouth ready to praise, a free spirit, and a life possessed only by your Son. And when Christ pries hell's fingers away from my heart, may he send me back home with a mercy story. It's in your Son's name that I pray.

Amen.

[1]Mark 4:39 [2]Mark 5:6-8 [3]Mark 5:12-13 [4]Mark 5:19-20

Day 22:
He Knows My Desperation

Scripture Reading: Mark 5:21-43

Meditation

Desperate people resort to desperate measures.

A synagogue leader named Jairus has a twelve-year-old daughter who's at death's door. There isn't much time. Soon death will turn the knob and swing open the door. The grim reaper will pick the little girl up, carry her into his tomb, and then slam the door in Jairus' face.

Jairus is running out of hope and his daughter is running out of time. He must get to Jesus and—somehow—he must get Jesus to come to his daughter. Desperation pushes Jairus toward Jesus; faith pulls him.

> *When he saw Jesus, he fell to his knees, beside himself as he begged, "My dear daughter is at death's door. Come and lay hands on her so she will get well and live." Jesus went with him, the whole crowd tagging along, pushing and jostling him.* [1]

Jesus doesn't say a word; he just begins to walk. He doesn't run. He doesn't stroll. He strides at a steady pace, with purpose. They're on their way but Jairus needs Jesus to hurry. The hands of death's clock move all so fast and yet Jesus' feet seem to move all too slow.

Not far from his house, Jairus' hopes are waylaid. Just when it seemed that all was going to be well, that death would have to wait many more years before it got his hands on this little girl, a hand of desperation reaches out from the crowd and touches the frayed hem of Jesus' garment. The touch stops him still in his stride.

A woman who had suffered a condition of hemorrhaging for twelve years—a long succession of physicians had treated her, and treated her badly, taking all her money and leaving her worse off than before—had heard about Jesus. She slipped in from behind and touched his robe. [2]

She's a desperate woman who is in dire straits. Like Jairus, she's run out of options.

For as long as Jairus' daughter has been alive, the woman has been hemorrhaging. She's gone to every doctor, taken every pill and—in the process—has spent all of her money. To add pain to misery, instead of getting better, she's gotten worse. Her desperation has turned into despair.

The best she can do now is to resort to a risk of faith. Popular belief has it that the power of a person is transmitted to his or her clothing. If she could only reach a finger out and graze the hem of Jesus' robe, maybe she might be able to snatch some of his power.

But even that's a risk. It's a risk because, according to the Mosaic Law, she's one of the unclean and anyone she touches becomes unclean too.

"If a woman has a discharge of blood for many days, but not at the time of her monthly period, or has a discharge that continues beyond the time of her period, she is unclean the same as during the time of her period. Every bed on which she lies during the time of the discharge and everything on which she sits becomes unclean the same as in her monthly period. Anyone who touches these things becomes unclean and must wash his clothes and bathe in water; he remains unclean until evening. [3]

Along with her daily loss of blood, she has lost the vital flow of her life. The religious leaders have ordered her to stay away from the synagogue, cutting her off from the lifeblood of worship. They have made it clear that a worshipper must be ritually clean in order to approach a Holy God.

They have also prohibited her from circulating within the community, isolating her in her pain. She's not to touch anyone. According to the Law, the unclean thing always defiles that which is clean. It never works the other way around—except with Jesus.

When the woman grabs ahold of Jesus' robe, power flows out of him and her bleeding stops. She has taken a risk of faith and her faith is rewarded.

Divinity isn't defiled. Her blood doesn't contaminate Jesus. Instead, Jesus cleanses her. He purges the plague from her body.

> *"Daughter, you took a risk of faith, and now you're healed and whole. Live well, live blessed! Be healed of your plague."* [4]

But the woman's breakthrough becomes Jairus' breaking point.

While Jesus was talking with the woman, the last sands of life in the little girl's hourglass ran out. News has just come from Jairus' house that his daughter is dead. The messengers tell the synagogue leader to stop bothering Jesus and to come back home, alone. But when Jesus overhears the conversation, he turns to Jairus and assures him that, though it might seem like it's too late, the Master is still right on time. Though things may have gone beyond desperation, there is no need to despair. They may have been interrupted, but it's a divine delay.

Jesus says to Jairus with a confident look,

"Don't listen to them; just trust me." [5]

Finally, Jesus reaches Jairus' house. He goes inside and confronts the crowd of professional mourners.

"Why all this busybody grief and gossip? This child isn't dead; she's sleeping." [6]

Jesus clears out the crowd, pulls only Peter, James, John, and the daughter's parents into the young girl's bedroom, and shuts the door behind them. When all is quiet, he clasps the girl's hands, tells her to get up, and then watches as the knob on death's door turns the other way. The hinges swing open and the little girl walks back into her parents' life.

Though late, Jesus is right on time.

Reflection

In what areas of your life have you reached a point of desperation? Has the desperation ever driven you to despair?

Have you ever felt unworthy to approach Christ? Why?

What does it feel like to take a risk of faith? How have you snuck through the crowd and stretched out a finger to touch the robe of Jesus?

Do you ever feel like the steps of Christ to your house are slowed by the needs of others? How do you deal with the delay?

Prayer

Father,

Like Jairus and the woman with the continuous hemorrhage, I am at a point of desperation. I've tried everything. I've seen everyone I know who could possibly help. I've gone everywhere and, instead of things getting better, they've gotten worse. I've run out of options and my desperation is turning into despair.

During this day, send me to the feet of Christ. Pull my hurt toward his heart. Empower me take a risk of faith. In my desperation, give me a humble plea that wets the dust, urgent feet that lead the way, an outstretched hand that gropes for a miraculous touch, attentive ears that listen only to the words of the Savior (and not the advice of the well meaning crowd), and a belief that beats fast though the Master walks slow. Remind me that, though the Master may be late, he's always on time. It's in his name that I pray.

Amen.

[1]Mark 5:22-24 [2]Mark 5:25-27 [3]Leviticus 15:25-27 [4]Mark 5:34 [5]Mark 5:36 [6]Mark 5:39

The Shelter
of Safety

"Even when the way goes
through Death Valley, I'm not
afraid when you walk at my side.
Your trusty shepherd's crook
makes me feel secure."

Psalm 23:4

The Good Shepherd knows that the journey home must pass through, not around, Death Valley. Though there may be many troubles, toils, and snares, the Shepherd charts a course for home and comforts his flock with the promise of his presence. When danger comes, he doesn't abandon the sheep; he runs to their side. And if enemies try to attack the flock, they'll have to deal with the long shank of the Shepherd's crook.

As you continue to walk with Christ during these forty days, reflect on the following ...

Reflection

When was the last time you walked the way of danger but didn't feel afraid?

What "Death Valleys" has the Shepherd led you safely through?

How does the Good Shepherd make you feel secure?

Day 23:
He Knows My Needs

Scripture Reading: Luke 11:1-13

Meditation

Though the disciples place their feet in the footprints of their Master, the ministry path they walk is rough-and-tumble. Each day of the journey has its own share of ankle turning trials and knee buckling anxiety. The road to the cross is replete with treacherous terrain, loose gravel, formidable obstacles, and forked passages. It's becoming painfully clear to the disciples that Christ followers aren't immune to trouble.

As the disciples march with Jesus toward Jerusalem, they worry about a multitude of every day needs: earthly provisions; heavenly protection; continual grace for ever-present trespasses; guidance through the valley of the shadow of death; and bulwarks against sin, flesh, and the devil.

Though the daily burdens of life are unwelcome guests, Jesus doesn't see them as intruders; he sees them as messengers carrying an invitation to bend the knee and fold the hands. In his eyes, every trial is an invitation to seize trouble by the throat, fold it into a petition, pack it into a prayer, and send it heavenward toward the Father.

But the disciples wonder about the God to whom they pray. They're not sure if the Creator of the universe is approachable or even concerned about the minute details of their every day life.

They wonder,

"Does he know about our needs? Does he care?
If he does care, is he willing to act?"

The disciples have heard others pray. Every time they go to the synagogue, they see religious leaders stand out in the open and bellow out formulaic prayers. These men and their prayers sound so pious. Like peacocks, the Pharisees puff out their chests and brag about their intercessory rituals—how much they pray, how long, how often.

Jesus had once told his disciples to beware of such displays of piety.

"The world is full of so-called prayer warriors who are prayer-ignorant. They're full of formulas and programs and advice, peddling techniques for getting what you want from God. Don't fall for that nonsense. This is your Father you are dealing with, and he knows better than you what you need. With a God like this loving you, you can pray very simply." [1]

When the disciples hear Jesus pray, they hear simplicity. The tone of his prayers is intimate. His words are passionate. When he prays, it's as if he's a little child talking to his Abba Father. Tender. Straightforward. No pretense or formality, just a child asking his daddy for the things that he needs.

After hearing Jesus pray so effortlessly, the disciples beg him to teach them how to pray. In a plain and informal way, Jesus begins,

"When you pray, say,

'Father,
Reveal who you are.
Set the world right.
Keep us alive with three square meals.
Keep us forgiven with you and forgiving others.
Keep us safe from ourselves and the Devil.' " [2]

Jesus' advice to his disciples is to keep it simple—if there's a need, simply ask and ask simply. No formulas. No gimmicks to get God to do what you want. No secret techniques.

He tells them: simply begin by saying, "Father"; believe that the Father in heaven cares more for you than you could ever care for your own; state all of your needs, those in heaven and those on earth; above all, be direct; and end with a hearty "Amen."

To illustrate his point, Jesus tells a story. A neighbor comes to his friend's house in the middle of the night and begins to pound on the door. He needs three loaves of bread because a friend has just arrived from out of town and his cupboards are bare. The friend inside the house tells the neighbor to go away. But the neighbor is persistent. He keeps knocking, waking up the entire house as well as all the neighbors. Finally, the man inside the house gets up, unlocks the door, and gives the man the three loaves of bread. Jesus says to his disciples,

"Ask and you'll get;
Seek and you'll find;
Knock and the door will open."

"Don't bargain with God. Be direct. Ask for what you need. This is not a cat-and-mouse, hide-and-seek game we're in. If your little boy asks for a serving of fish, do you scare him with a live snake on his plate? If your little girl asks for an egg, do you trick her with a spider? As bad as you are, you wouldn't think of such a thing— you're at least decent to your own children. And don't you think the Father who conceived you in love will give the Holy Spirit when you ask him?" 3

When the disciples have a need, Jesus tells them to pray. He tells them to lift earthly troubles to heaven's gates, not because they need to inform the Father in heaven of their needs but because—in the praying—the children come to know that they have a heavenly Father, one who knows their every need and is ready and willing to act.

Ask. Seek. Knock. The Father, to whom Jesus prays, loves to answer.

Reflection

What's the difference between wants and needs? What wants do you have? What needs?

How do you view prayer? Is it a means by which you inform God about yours needs or—in praying—do you come to know the heart of the Father?

How is Jesus inviting you to be bolder in your prayer life?

Jesus said to ask, seek, and knock. Write a prayer stating your needs. Be direct. Don't bargain with God. Simply ask and ask simply.

Prayer

Father,

I am prayer-ignorant. All too many times my prayers are full of formulas, complex rituals, manipulating techniques, and bartering tactics for getting you to do what I want. When I pray, I spend the majority of my time informing you of my troubles. Yet, in my need, you ask me to keep it simple, to be direct, to pray out of an intimate relationship with you and not out of a hollow ritual.

During this day, remind me that you are a perfect Father and that you care more about my needs than I do. In Christ, help me pray relationally. Let me call you "Abba", "Daddy", "Father". Through Christ, help me pray rightly. Your will. Your way. Your time. On account of Christ, help me pray boldly. No request unspoken. No desire left unsaid. In your Son's name I pray.

Amen

Day 24:

He Knows My Hypocrisy

Scripture Reading: Luke 11:37−12:3

Meditation

As Jesus finishes talking to the crowd about the mood of the current age—proof appetites, curiosity cravings, and miracle meals—a religious leader pushes his way from the center of the pack of people to the front.

When he's within earshot of Jesus, the religious leader shouts over the buzz of the crowd, inviting him to come to his home for dinner. Jesus hears the request, makes eye contact with the man, and honors it by nodding his head. Then the man stands on his tiptoes and points the way over the heads of the crowd. Jesus follows him home.

Jesus' host prides himself on being one of the Pharisees. This influential religious ruling party is known as "the set apart ones", spiritual separatists who have pledged themselves to obeying not only all the facets of the Mosaic Law but also the accompanying oral tradition of the elders.

For the Pharisee, Torah and the oral tradition of the elders are laid side-by-side, equal in authority, coequal as sources of truth. This oral tradition holds a high place in the Pharisee's life because it not only interprets the Law, it prescribes in exacting detail acceptable and forbidden daily behavior.

According to the interpretation of the elders, God's grace extends only to those who keep the Law of Moses. Salvation comes through doing that which is good and not doing that which is evil.

The Pharisee who invites Jesus to share his table holds tight to these rules and regulations. Day by day, he's driven to attain a righteousness that comes through the Law. He shuns anything and anyone that would make him unclean. Because he believes that salvation is at stake, he's a stickler for ceremonial purity. For the Pharisee, cleanliness is not next to godliness; it is godliness.

As the host opens his house to Jesus, he stays true to his beliefs. He performs the required religious rituals. Ceremonial cleanliness is his obsession, especially before dinner.

The Pharisees—Jews in general, in fact—would never eat a meal without going through the motions of a ritual hand-washing, with an especially vigorous scrubbing if they had just come from the market (to say nothing of the scourings they'd give jugs and pots and pans). [1]

As everyone moves toward the dinner table, the Pharisee, as is his custom, takes some water from one of the ceremonial jars standing in the corner and pours it over his hands. Since he's just fought his way through a throng of people, he gives his hands an especially vigorous scrubbing.

Any number of things in the crowd might have defiled him: the carcass of a creeping thing in the middle of the road, the stain of blood on someone's cloak, a brush with the immoral, a bump up against someone with an infectious disease. He lives by the belief that salvation comes through constant and clean works. And so, before he sits down to eat, he washes. He rinses. He washes again. The squeaky-clean of his pruned hands is only matched by the sparkle of the plates on the table.

While the Pharisee scrubs his hands, Jesus bypasses the ceremonial washing jars and goes directly to the table. When the Pharisee turns around, he's shocked to see Jesus seated, hands folded, dry and dirty. He's offended that Jesus would so blatantly disregard the tradition of the elders. After all, if he is a

Teacher, he should wash. Failure to wash is tantamount to sin and sin is separation from God. But when it comes to sin, Jesus looks beyond the water that washes the dirt of the hands. He looks deep into the heart.

True, the Pharisee has gone to great lengths to keep his religious hands clean. But upon inspection, Jesus notices that, though the outside of the Pharisee's sanctimonious house has curb appeal, the foundations it sits on are rotting away.

Jesus looks past the outward show of the Pharisee's piety and burrows deep to the inward reality—heartless religiosity. In seeing the Pharisee, he remembers the revelation of Isaiah and the prophet's pointed words hit the mark.

> *"These people make a big show of saying the right*
> *thing, but their heart isn't in it.*
> *They act like they are worshiping me,*
> *but they don't mean it."* [2]

The Pharisee's house may have religion but it's a religion without the heart of God. There is no beat of grace in the Pharisee's piety. No flow of mercy. Instead there is only play-acting worship: hollow words for hallowed things; spiritual masks that display counterfeit sincerity. When it comes to the daily expectations of the common man, the Pharisee is a religious taskmaster. He walks around with a puffed out chest and puffed up ego. The Pharisee might look religious, but it's all a sham. He's a fraud, a phony. And Jesus calls him on it.

*"I know you Pharisees burnish the surface of your cups
and plates so they sparkle in the sun, but I also know
your insides are maggoty with greed and secret evil.
Stupid Pharisees! Didn't the One who made the outside
also make the inside? Turn both your pockets and your
hearts inside out and give generously to the poor; then
your lives will be clean, not just your dishes and your
hands."* 3

Such hypocrisy is devil's yeast, invading and pervading all
that is good and godly. As Jesus leaves the man's house, he
warns his disciples to stay away from the leaven of Pharisee
phoniness.

*"Watch yourselves carefully so you don't get contaminated
with Pharisee yeast, Pharisee phoniness. You can't keep
your true self hidden forever; before long you'll be exposed.
You can't hide behind a religious mask forever; sooner or
later the mask will slip and your true face will be known.
You can't whisper one thing in private and preach the
opposite in public; the day's coming when those whispers
will be repeated all over town."* 4

True religion wears no mask; it only reflects the face
of Christ.

Reflection

When was the last time you put on a good religious show but your heart wasn't in it?

What yeast of hypocrisy is subtly pervading your life? In what ways do you look good on the outside—while on the inside—you're filled with evil desires?

How has Christ exposed your true self to his grace and mercy? What does it feel like to live a consistent life, inside and out?

In what ways does your spiritual life reflect the face of Christ?

Prayer

Father,

The yeast of hypocrisy has subtly pervaded my life. My worship is hollow. My faith is heartless. The beat of grace has slowed and the flow of mercy has been reduced to a trickle. When the lights are on, I put on a good religious show but, behind the scenes, my heart isn't in it. I wear a mask and hide behind the covering of the law but my mask is slipping and my sin is beginning to show.

During this day, cleanse from me the inside out so that what is in my heart might be reflective of what I do with my hands. Remove whatever yeast of hypocrisy might be in my life and replace it with the leaven of your Son's grace. May his forgiveness pervade my life so that I might rise up and become a new creation, shining and sparkling from the inside out. It's in Christ's name that I pray.

Amen.

[1]Mark 7:3-4 [2]Mark 7:6-7 [3]Luke 11:39-41 [4]Luke 12:1-3

Day 25:
He Knows My Anxiety

Scripture Reading: Luke 12:13-34

Meditation

An unwieldy crowd of thousands follows Jesus. In the middle of the shoving and the toe stepping are two brothers at each other's throats. Greed has a stranglehold on them.

The two are obsessed with the equitable division of their dead father's possessions and one of them thinks that his sibling's proposed split is unfair. After looking at the slice of the inheritance that he was served, he compared it to his brother's. Convinced that his is the smaller piece, he's demanded that the case be taken to one of the rabbis for arbitration. As Jesus passes, the slighted brother yells out for a hearing.

"Teacher, order my brother to give me a fair share of the family inheritance."

He replied, "Mister, what makes you think it's any of my business to be a judge or mediator for you?" [1]

Though religious teachers were often consulted in such civic matters and had the power to render verdicts, Jesus passes on pronouncing a judgment. He's not concerned about the fine print in the will. He's concerned about the underlying motive behind the brothers' dispute:

"Why would kin go for the jugular? What's boiling their blood? What possible gain would be worth losing a brother?"

Looking to reveal the deeper issues, Jesus denies the request for legal resolution. Instead, he uses the request to give a ruling on the real nature of life. He weighs in on the place and purpose of possessions, the vice grip of anxiety on the human heart, the futility of worry, the ultimate source of security, and the intimate and timely care of an attentive God.

> *Speaking to the people, he went on, "Take care! Protect yourself against the least bit of greed. Life is not defined by what you have, even when you have a lot."* [2]

Jesus then told the crowd a story about a rich farmer. The man had planned well for his retirement but had failed to prepare for eternity. He had filled his barns with Self and not with God. Excess had become his source of solace, financial security his idol of worship. But in his quest for abundance, he failed to learn the lesson of Solomon:

> *"And I hated everything I'd accomplished and accumulated on this earth. I can't take it with me—no, I have to leave it to whoever comes after me. Whether they're worthy or worthless—and who's to tell?—they'll take over the earthly results of my intense thinking and hard work. Smoke."* [3]

When death carries life away, the barns are left behind.

Turning his back to the crowd, Jesus begins to talk to his disciples. He empties their barns of Self and fills them back up with God. As he cleans house, he redefines what life is all about: self-worth is not equivalent to net worth; the value of a life dare not be measured by the amount of valuables; possessions are simply possessions and not obsessions; and where the heart is, there is the treasure. To those whose hearts are choked by anxiety, Jesus begins to loosen the stranglehold of worry.

> *"Don't fuss about what's on the table at mealtimes or if the clothes in your closet are in fashion. There is far more to your inner life than the food you put in your stomach, more to your outer appearance than the clothes you hang on your body. Look at the ravens, free and unfettered, not tied down to a job description, carefree in the care of God. And you count far more."* [4]

Though there may be needs, Jesus tells his disciples not to worry. After all, what can worry accomplish? It can't add hours to the day nor money to the bank account. Anxiety is nothing more than a busybody doing busy work. It meddles in the mind, pries its way into the heart, feeds off of fear, expends emotional energy, consumes valuable time, but produces no dividends.

> *"Has anyone by fussing before the mirror ever gotten taller by so much as an inch? If fussing can't even do that, why fuss at all? Walk into the fields and look at the wildflowers. They don't fuss with their appearance—but have you ever seen color and design quite like it? The ten best-dressed men and women in the country look shabby alongside them. If God gives such attention to the wild-flowers, most of them never even seen, don't you think he'll attend to you, take pride in you, do his best for you?"* [5]

Jesus' answer to anxiety is the assurance that the Father is paying attention. If the Father takes the time to attend to the birds of the air and the fading wildflowers of the field, how much more does he keep a watchful eye on the needs of his children?

Jesus is trying to get his disciples to relax, to release their white-knuckle grip on the possessions of life. He wants them to place palms up and open toward heaven because when the hands are clutched, they're not able to receive.

> *"What I'm trying to do here is get you to relax, not be so preoccupied with getting so you can respond to God's giving. People who don't know God and the way he works fuss over these things, but you know both God and how he works. Steep yourself in God-reality, God-initiative, God-provisions. You'll find all your everyday human concerns will be met. Don't be afraid of missing out. You're my dearest friends! The Father wants to give you the very kingdom itself."* [6]

Jesus has made his point. Life is more than food or fashion. It's more than quantity of goods, quality of life, or stockpiled security. It's ultimately about the inheritance of eternity disbursed to the children of God through grace, day by day. The treasure isn't in a barn full of temporary possessions. It's in a person. It's in him. He's the one who pays close attention to the intimate issues of life. He's the one who attends to daily needs. He's the antidote for anxiety.

Reflection

Is there any anxiety that has a stranglehold on your heart? What's the source of the uneasiness?

How is Jesus trying to get you to relax so that you're not so preoccupied with getting but rather can respond to his giving?

What does it feel like to be freed up so that you can devote full attention to the kingdom of God?

How do you define the value of your life? Where's your treasure? In what ways is God showing you that you count more that the birds of the air or the flowers of the field?

Prayer

Father,

Anxiety has a stranglehold on my heart. I am preoccupied with getting, keeping, preserving, protecting, and storing possessions rather than on occupying myself with you, the Giver of all good gifts. My anxiety reveals my treasure—Self. And my treasure reveals my god—Self Sufficiency.

During this day, help me shun the false security of possessions and embrace the reality of being possessed by you. Empty my barns of anything that may point to Self and fill them with your Son. Bury the treasure of grace deep within my heart, safe from thieves and robbers. Open my hands so that I might receive the inheritance of heaven, day by day. And when I receive, help me give. I want all that you have for my life. In the name of Jesus I pray.

Amen.

[1]Luke 12:14 [2]Luke 12:15 [3]Ecclesiastes 2:18-19 [4]Luke 12:23-24
[5]Luke 12:25-28 [6]Luke 12:29-32

Day 26:
He Knows My Separation
Scripture Reading: Luke 17:11-19

Meditation

Living outside of a village, in the borderland between Galilee and Samaria, is a man who bears a double curse. By birth he's a Samaritan and by lot he's a leper. He's not morally responsible for either but both his lineage and his disease bring with them the sentence of a ceremonial curse—separation.

According to strict social and religious norms, Jews aren't supposed to associate with Samaritans. The Jews consider the dogs of Samaria to be religious half-breeds, a defiled mix of Jewish and mongrel blood spilled over from the Assyrian captivity.

Fueling the animosity between the two is the fact that the Samaritans had adopted the foreign gods of the Assyrian invaders and had mingled them with the God of Abraham, Isaac, and Jacob. The result? They offered up polluted worship to Yahweh. The Samaritans even went so far as to build their own temple on Mt. Gerazim, spurning Jerusalem as the true place of worship.

So despised are the Samaritans that pious Jews traveling from Galilee to Jerusalem make the long journey around Samaria instead of taking the chance of defiling themselves by passing through Samaritan territory.

Because of his debased lineage, the Jews in the area label the Samaritan an "outsider." They forbid him to worship in Jerusalem. Ceremonially they separate him from God, severing him from the hand of mercy, and cutting him off from the gift of grace.

As if spiritual segregation isn't enough, the man's leprosy widens the span of the man's separation. According to the Levitical Law, whoever has an infectious disease is declared to be "unclean" and is to be separated from the rest of the community.

> *"The person with such an infectious disease must wear torn clothes, let his hair be unkempt, cover the lower part of his face and cry out, 'Unclean! Unclean!' As long as he has the infection he remains unclean. He must live alone; he must live outside the camp."* [1]

As part of their religious duties, the priests serve as public health officers in the community. They police the community for anything that could cause the "chosen and set apart ones of Israel" to become unclean. The sanctity of the community has to be protected at all costs. The good of the many outweighs the needs of the one. For the sake of ceremonial holiness, the unclean thing has to be cast out.

Because of his disease, the leper is designated by society as one of the "unclean." His peers have sequestered him from the rest of the community, mandating that he live outside the village, isolated and alone in his pain.

But where there is misery, there is company. Living outside of the village with him is a colony of lepers, a community of outcasts made up of both Jews and Samaritans. What social barriers race had erected, leprosy has now tore down. The hideous disease has made them equals: equal in pain, coequal in despair. Leprosy is their common bond. Piece by piece, each one of their lives is falling apart. Men who were once alienated from one another by race, are now kin—brothers in misery.

Their disease has removed them from their proper place in society. They are the "marginal people": individuals forced to stand at a distance around the rim of the community—part of the periphery, never the center.

Besides eating away at their lives, their disease has devoured their faith. They have given up praying for such specific requests as an arrest of the disease's cancerous appetite, restoration of digits and reformation of the face, a return to the family and the life they once had, or the warmth of a compassionate touch. Their only cry is for mercy. And where there is a plea for mercy, heaven's Son answers.

When it's time for Jesus to go to the cross, he intentionally steps over the border between Galilee and Samaria and marches his way through the Samaritan territory toward Jerusalem. He ignores all of the existing social prohibitions and comes near to those who are far away. His grace extends beyond Judaism.

Salvation is walking through Samaria.

When the lepers see him coming, they run out to meet him. Per the requirements of the Law, they keep their proper distance but bridge the required ceremonial gulf by yelling over and over again,

"Jesus, Master, have mercy on us!" [2]

Jesus raises his hands to shield his eyes from the sun. After getting a good look at them he cups his hands, places them around his mouth, and shouts back,

"Go, show yourselves to the priests." [3]

Such a command is good news. Standing before the priest is the first step toward regaining a good standing within the community. The ten, not yet healed, go quickly to the priests. It's only while they're on their way that they all become clean. Toes and fingers are restored. Flesh returns to their faces. Numbness wears off and sensations surge throughout their bodies.

When they realize that they are healed, one of them—the Samaritan—stops in mid stride. He turns around, leaving the other nine running toward the priest, and returns to Jesus. All the way back, he shouts his hallelujahs.

This time there will be no separation between him and Jesus. He will not stand a shout away. Jesus has made him clean. Worship has to be given face-to-face. The Samaritan rushes to Jesus' feet and kneels as he worships, continually thanking him for his mercy. Sweet mercy.

Perplexed that only one had returned out of the ten, Jesus asks,

> *"Were not ten healed? Where are the nine? Can none be found to come back and give glory to God except this out-sider?" Then he said to him, "Get up. On your way. Your faith has healed and saved you."* [4]

The man with the double curse receives a double blessing: health and salvation. Christ has come near. Mercy has closed the gap. There is no longer any separation between man and God.

Reflection

In what ways are you shouting from a distance for Jesus to help you?

When was the last time you cried out, *"Jesus, Master, have mercy on me!"*?

How are you like the one leper that returned to give thanks? How are you like the nine that kept running?

What act of Christ has stopped you in your stride, turned you around, and brought you back to his feet shouting gratitude and glorifying God?

Prayer

Father,

Like the Samaritan leper, my life is falling apart. Sin's cancerous appetite has consumed every part of my being: body, emotions, relationships, and faith. I confess that I am full of sin and am suffering the just consequences of my transgressions. Therefore, I do not presume to utter, and am long past asking for, any specific request. My only plea is for mercy. As I stand at a distance and shout out, I pray that the eyes of your Son might look upon my condition and that, when he sees my need, he will come near.

During this day, show me all of the ways that Christ has stepped into my territory. Assure me that he went to the cross to bridge the gap between my sin and his salvation. Whenever he removes the leprosy that eats at my life, may my legs sprint toward him. While others run along on their own way, happy to be healed but not grateful to God, bring me to your Son. When I approach him, open my mouth to give thanks, not from a distance, but face to face. In the name of Christ I pray.

Amen.

[1]Leviticus 13:45-46 [2]Luke 17:13 [3]Luke 17:14 [4]Luke 17:17-19

Day 27:

He Knows My Tendency
To Play It Safe

Scripture Reading: Matthew 25:14-30

Meditation

When it comes to extending the kingdom of God, Jesus never played it safe. Throughout his ministry, there has never been any caution in his steps, only the determination to live all out for the purpose of his Father—nothing held back, all given. But living such a life is risky. It brings with it both rewards from heaven and consequences on earth.

From the very beginning of his ministry, Jesus has gone against the social mores of his culture and has raised the ire of the religious leaders. For the sake of the kingdom, he's embraced the social outcast, daring to approach the unapproachable. He's ignored ceremonial etiquette, frequently breaking the rules of the Sabbath for the sake of those who need true rest. He has gone out of his way to enfold the spiritually unclean, having the audacity to extend grace to the grace-less, bringing the kingdom of God to the lost sheep outside of the flock of Israel.

In these last days, he's courageously made his way to Jerusalem. In this city, he will risk it all. He'll stretch out his arms and go out on a limb for all of humanity. Though death awaits him, he refuses to live cautiously.

His Father has promised him that after the cross will come the resurrection. When the vault of the tomb opens, he will see his redemptive investment pay out eternal dividends: victory over sin, death, and the power of the devil.

For forty days after his resurrection, Jesus will give proof of his resurrection. When the time for his ascension draws near, he'll take another risk. He'll entrust the Gospel into the hands of his disciples, ordinary men without formal education in the Scriptures, schooled only at his feet. Afterwards he'll be taken up and disappear into the clouds, hidden from their sight yet always present. Added to the promise of his presence is a guarantee; one day he will reappear.

While they wait, the disciples are to watch.

> *"So stay awake, alert. You have no idea what day your Master will show up. But you do know this: You know that if the homeowner had known what time of night the burglar would arrive, he would have been there with his dogs to prevent the break-in. Be vigilant just like that. You have no idea when the Son of Man is going to show up."* [1]

As Jesus prepares his disciples for the time when he'll no longer be visibly among them, he paints five pictures in parables. Collectively, the parables are framed around the theme of watchfulness. Each individual parable brings a deeper dimension to the whole. As Jesus teaches, he paints with vigorous strokes.

> *"Keep your eyes open! Watch the skies! Be prepared! I might show up when you least expect it! While you wait, get busy and stay busy with kingdom work!"*

Jesus has expectations. While his disciples wait, they are to work. When he ascends into the clouds, he's going to give them the keys of the kingdom. Though he'll always be the owner of the house, they're going to be appointed the managers—stewards of his grace and the gifts of the Holy Spirit.

So that they might remember their calling and be diligent in their duties, Jesus tells the story of a master and three of his servants.

> *"It's also like a man going off on an extended trip. He called his servants together and delegated responsibilities. To one he gave five thousand dollars, to another two thousand, to a third one thousand, depending on their abilities. Then he left. Right off, the first servant went to work and doubled his master's investment. The second did the same. But the man with the single thousand dug a hole and carefully buried his master's money."* [2]

As the master is about to go off on an extended trip, he calls three of his servants and entrusts them with cash assets, each according to his ability. He knows their potential. He's carefully watched and monitored their capacity to perform. He gives each one of them no more than he can handle and no less than he needs to fulfill his responsibility. There is no parity in the allowance but there is equity—just and reasonable allotment in keeping with the gifts of the servants. The master gives them the charge to manage things well while he is away and then leaves.

The first two servants rush out straightaway and put their master's money to work. They work hard and double their master's investment. But the third digs a hole and buries his master's money. After a long delay, the master returns and calls his servants to settle up accounts. The first two servants rush to the master and show him how they have doubled his investment.

He commends both of them,

> *"Good work! You did your job well. From now on be my partner."* [3]

But the third servant comes with a handful of dirty money and a bag full of excuses. He accuses his master of being overly demanding, loving high standards, and hating careless ways. He explains that he didn't want to incur his master's wrath and so he chose to play it safe. He had buried his master's investment and now he returns it to him as is. No more than when he got it. No less. The master is furious.

> *"That's a terrible way to live! It's criminal to live cautiously like that! If you knew I was after the best, why did you do less than the least? The least you could have done would have been to invest the sum with the bankers, where at least I would have gotten a little interest."*

> *"Take the thousand and give it to the one who risked the most. And get rid of this 'play-it-safe' who won't go out on a limb. Throw him out into utter darkness."* [4]

While Jesus, the Master, is hidden from their sight, he calls his servants to watch, wait, and work. There is no time to play it safe. The currency of grace is to be invested until the very last minute of time. Eternal dividends are at stake.

Nothing ventured for the kingdom ... nothing gained.

Reflection

What is the posture of your life while you wait for the Master to reappear? Are you active or passive?

What type of kingdom responsibilities has the Master entrusted to you? Are you playing it safe or are you working diligently?

In what ways have you doubled the Master's investments? How have you buried your kingdom talents?

When the Master reappears and settles accounts, what do you think he will say to you?

Prayer

Father,

Your Son took a great risk when he entrusted the work of the kingdom into the hands of men. While we wait for his reappearance, he has called us not only to watch with anticipation but also to work with diligence. I must confess that, during the delay, I have become passive. There have been many times, when, out of fear or laziness, I have buried the kingdom investment that your Son entrusted to me.

During this day, remind me that your Son knows my abilities and that he only asks me to steward that which I am able. No more than I can. No less than I am capable. Help me to live courageously: doing what I can, when I can, with what I have. Embolden me to take risks of grace and invest myself in the economy of the kingdom of God. May your Spirit double my efforts so that I might one day present them before the Master and hear him say, *"Good work! You did your job well. From now on be my partner."* It's in the Master's name I pray.

Amen.

[1]Matthew 24:42-44 [2]Matthew 25:14-18 [3]Matthew 25:23 [4]Matthew 25:26-30

Day 28:
He Knows My Worship

Scripture Reading: Mark 12:38-44

Meditation

Soon Jesus will offer himself up as the once and for all sacrifice for sin. As he prepares to take the final steps to the cross, he goes to the temple courts and finds a quiet place to sit. He positions himself so that his eyes can see and his ears can hear the sights and sounds of worship. From his vantage point, he notices everything.

He hears the bleating of lambs. A sacrifice is about to be offered. Blood will be shed. Sin will be atoned for. With every lamb's cry, the Lamb of God winces. The prophetic words of Isaiah cut deep.

> *"We're all like sheep who've wandered off*
> *and gotten lost.*
> *We've all done our own thing, gone our own way.*
> *And God has piled all our sins, everything we've*
> *done wrong, on him, on him.*
> *He was beaten, he was tortured,*
> *but he didn't say a word.*
> *Like a lamb taken to be slaughtered*
> *and like a sheep being sheared,*
> *he took it all in silence."* [1]

Returning his attention to the activity in the temple courts, Jesus takes note of the Pharisees. As the "set apart ones", they believe that their lives revolve around rigid and complete obedience to the Law of Moses. In addition to the Old Testament Law, the Pharisees have added their own interpretations and traditions—613 clear statutes in the Law, 365 prohibitions and 248 exhortations.

For the Pharisee, worship has evolved into a complex list of prescribed rules and rituals. Intimacy with the Almighty has been replaced with religious activity. Again, Jesus hears the prophets speak.

> *"I'm after love that lasts, not more religion.*
> *I want you to know God, not go to more prayer*
> *meetings."* [2]

Jesus glares at the Pharisees. In a crowd, these spiritual peacocks aren't hard to find. They're the ones dressed in long, white, linen robes, looking and playing the part of religious leaders. As they strut through the temple grounds, they bellow long-winded prayers, looking for and loving the attention. This isn't worship; it's a religious show. But it's not anything new. What the prophets had talked about centuries earlier, Jesus sees played out in real time.

> *"Do you think all God wants are sacrifices—*
> *empty rituals just for show?*
> *He wants you to listen to him!*
> *Plain listening is the thing,*
> *not staging a lavish religious production."* [3]

The Pharisees are the main players in this lavish production. As they strut around the temple courts in their flowing robes, they steal center stage from the very God they claim to worship. They're only acting pious and play-acting at worship. All of their preening behavior boils down to ecclesiastical spectacle. It's hypocrisy dressed in pretentious clothing.

Jesus calls his disciples over and warns them to keep an eye out for such spiritual over acting.

"Watch out for the religion scholars. They love to walk around in academic gowns, preening in the radiance of public flattery, basking in prominent positions, sitting at the head table at every church function. And all the time they are exploiting the weak and helpless. The longer their prayers, the worse they get. But they'll pay for it in the end." [4]

Once more Jesus turns his attention to the sights and sounds of worship. He listens as the wealthy throw handfuls of copper coins into one of the thirteen trumpet-shaped receptacles placed in the courtyard. Their offering for the temple treasury sounds impressive as it rattles around in the containers. When totaled, however, it's just a lot of loose pocket change thrown in to make a lot of noise.

As Jesus reflects on the state of worship in the temple courts, his heart is grieved. Outward signs of worship abound, but when he looks beneath the surface, he sees only hollow ritualistic shells: no heart. All the proper forms of worship are there—sacrifices, prayers, and offerings—but none of its substance. There is no spirit or truth. No giving of all to the Father. There may be plenty of sacrificial lambs and copper coins, but there aren't any living sacrifices of praise.

Just when the temple courts seem to be void of true worship, Jesus finds a picture of intimacy with the Almighty in the most unlikely place. In the midst of all of the religious noise, a poor widow walks up to one of the receptacles and drops in two small copper coins, worth only a fraction of a cent. As the coins tumble into the temple treasury, they barely make a sound. But Jesus hears her act of worship. It isn't the sound of her offering that catches his attention; it's the thunderous beat of her heart. Seeing her sacrifice, Jesus says to his disciples,

"The truth is that this poor widow gave more to the collection than all the others put together. All the others gave what they'll never miss; she gave extravagantly what she couldn't afford—she gave her all." [5]

Compared to the gifts of the rich, her offering barely made a noise. But her act of worship was so valuable that the angels trumpeted its worth throughout heaven. It was given out of poverty. It was true sacrifice: all of her for all of her God. As Jesus looks at the widow's sacrifice, he smiles. Soon, at the cross, he'll do the same.

Reflection

If Christ were to sit in the sanctuary and watch your worship, what would he see?

In what ways are you like the poor widow? What are the two small coins that you can place in the temple treasury as your act of worship?

Have you made lots of noise with your worship, only later to admit that it was void of substance?

What is your sacrifice of praise?

Prayer

Father,

I confess that my worship is often full of empty rituals. I haven't worshiped you with all my passion, intelligence, and energy and I certainly haven't loved others as myself. My sacrifice of praise has made a lot of noise but it's void of substance. It draws more attention to me than adoration toward you.

During this day, give me the heart of the poor widow. Humble me. Show me that my only wealth is in your Son, Jesus the Christ. Open my heart and release my hands in worship to give all that I have for all that you are. May I do all of this in secret, not for public show. And remind me that the smallest act of worship done with the right heart is far greater than all of the offerings and sacrifices of men. Remind me that, though no one else is aware of my actions, Christ is. And when he sees such faith, he directs all of heaven's attention toward me. It's in your Son's name that I pray.

Amen.

[1]Isaiah 53:6-7 [2]Hosea 6:6 [3]1 Samuel 15:22 [4]Mark 12:38-40 [5]Mark 12:43-44

The Shelter
of Celebration

"You serve me a six-course dinner
right in front of my enemies. You
revive my drooping head; my cup
brims with blessing."

Psalm 23:5

When the sheep can't seem to go the "second-mile", the Good Shepherd stops in enemy territory, sets up a protective perimeter, and revives his flock with an all out spread. His hospitality goes beyond expectations: six-course dinner right in front of the enemy; soothing oil for the head; blessings flowing over the brim. With the Shepherd as host, there is no lack of good things. Fed and well rested, the flock follows as the Shepherd leads on.

As you feast with Christ during these forty days, reflect on the following ...

Reflection

When was the last time you felt like you couldn't go the "second-mile"?

How has Christ nourished you beyond expectation?

In what ways do you have blessings flowing over the brim?

He Knows My Plotting

Scripture Reading: John 11:38-57

Meditation

After four days dead, Lazarus is now alive. Jesus, the Resurrection and the Life, had finally arrived. With his face still wet from a stream of tears, Jesus had made his way to the middle of the graveyard, ordered the stone rolled away, and had shouted out his beloved friend's name.

"Lazarus, come out!" [1]

When Jesus spoke Lazarus' name, death let loose its grip, the breath of life returned, and Lazarus—still wrapped in burial clothes from toes to neck—sat up and baby stepped his way out of the tomb.

It was an undeniable God-sign. All who were there had seen the glory of God. The evidence was clear; Jesus had to be the sent Son of the Father, the Resurrection and the Life. But where the glory of God shines—there, in the shadows—evil men begin to scheme.

For some of the Jews—those who came from Jerusalem to comfort Lazarus' two sisters—the miracle was the beginning of a spiritual turnaround. They saw what Jesus did, recognized the glory of God, put their faith in Jesus, and began to follow him.

For others, a cadaver walking out of the tomb after days of death sleep was a spiritual turn-off. They didn't dare deny the reality of the miracle but they misread its intended meaning. They saw it only as a well-orchestrated publicity stunt performed to gain a political following. These few ran back to Jerusalem, found the Pharisees, and told all about Jesus.

Unsettled about the developing events in Bethany, the Pharisees call an emergency meeting of the Sanhedrin, the Jewish ruling body. After hearing the report, they all agree that a dead man walking around is more than a miracle; it's a death threat to Israel's very way of life. The fear is that Jesus will use this God-sign as a political rallying point and stage a revolution against Rome. Resurrection of the dead is one thing; revolution is another. If Rome is provoked, Jewish blood will freely flow through Jerusalem; there will be far more Jews going into graves than those who miraculously come out. The good of the nation is at stake. This Jesus must be stopped.

The number one question for the Sanhedrin is: What to do with Jesus? For the sake of the nation of Israel, something has to be done about this religious renegade. The good of the many must come before the political motives of the one.

> *"What do we do now?" they asked. "This man keeps on doing things, creating God-signs. If we let him go on, pretty soon everyone will be believing in him and the Romans will come and remove what little power and privilege we still have."* [2]

All of the members of the Jewish ruling body realize that resistance against Rome is futile. Caesar and his legions already have a stranglehold on the nation. Why give them any incentive to go for the jugular? Political wisdom suggests that it would be best for Israel to keep calm rather than to call any attention to itself. Rome must be kept at a distance. Keep Caesar happy and then Israel can retain what little power and privilege it still has.

Clearly then, for the good of people, Jesus must be silenced. With the threat outlined and the objective clear, Caiphas, the Chief Priest, proposes a sacrificial scheme.

"Don't you know anything? Can't you see that it's to our advantage that one man dies for the people rather than the whole nation be destroyed?" He didn't say this of his own accord, but as Chief Priest that year he unwittingly prophesied that Jesus was about to die sacrificially for the nation, and not only for the nation but so that all God's exile-scattered children might be gathered together into one people. [3]

As Caiphas schemes, he speaks more than he knows.

As Chief Priest, his words are filled with a prophetic double meaning. On the surface, they reveal the plotting of an evil man who misunderstands the person and work of the Messiah. But beneath the surface is another revelation: the redemptive plan of God.

Unwittingly, Caiphas speaks forth salvation's plan. Jesus will die sacrificially for the people but it won't be for political reasons. Rome will still come. Jerusalem will be destroyed. But the death of the Christ will still save the people, not from the sword of the infidel but from the sting of sin, death, and the Evil One. Unconscious and unaware of the true import of his words, Caiphas declares good news through an evil scheme.

As Jesus begins his march to the cross, his Father assures him that, come what may, heaven will have its way. The Almighty is the God of the great reversal. As the Father has always done, he will take the destructive schemes of men, spin them around on their heels, and turn them in a new direction. Just as the Father worked all things together for the good of Joseph in Egypt, he now promises to do the same for his own Son.

"Don't you see, you planned evil against me but God used those same plans for my good, as you see all around you right now—life for many people." [4]

Human plots can't thwart the Father's divine plan. They will always end up walking hand in hand with his redemptive purposes. What men intend for evil, the Father will work out for good. The cross will become the great reversal; one man's death will bring life for many people.

"Don't you know anything? Can't you see that it's to our advantage that one man dies for the people rather than the whole nation be destroyed?" [5]

Reflection

Caiphas, the high priest, prophesied that it would be good for one man to die sacrificially for all of the people. Why is that good news?

How has God taken something in your life that men intended for evil and turned it into something good?

When was the last time God took one of your schemes and turned it around to accomplish his salvation plan?

How is the sacrifice of Christ at the cross the great reversal?

Prayer

Father,

When I see God-signs, I don't always believe. Instead I misread your Son's motives and begin to scheme. Like Caiphas, I plot to take care of myself, planning ways to survive, even if that means silencing your Son.

During this day, remind me that you are the God who takes plans intended for evil and turns them around to accomplish good. Assure me, that although I scheme the worst for your Son, he still wants the best for me. As I gaze upon the sacrifice of your Son, show me the true meaning behind the cross. Open the eyes of my heart to see that the crucifixion was for me ... because of me. Send your Holy Spirit to give me faith to take hold of all that Christ offers. Today, may I come to embrace the heavenly revelation under Caiphas' scheme, *"... it's to our advantage that one man dies for the people..."* It's in your Son's name that I pray.

Amen.

[1]John 11:43 [2]John 11:47-48 [3]John 11:49-52 [4]Genesis 50:20 [5]John 11:49-50

He Knows My Betrayal

Scripture Reading: Matthew 26:17-30

Meditation

For Jesus, the time of treachery is near.

In a few hours he will be betrayed into the hands of sinful men. A cabal of religious leaders will deride and persecute him. They will prosecute him with a mock trial and render a contrived verdict of blasphemy. Then they will march him to Pilate and demand that Jesus be sentenced to a criminal's death—crucifixion.

That all of this is to happen is no surprise. The Scripture has made it clear. The Lamb of God will be sacrificed. At the cross, the angel of death will pass over the transgressions of the world so that an eternal Exodus might occur: freedom from sin; a passage through death; and a release from the bondage of the Devil. The redemptive path is well marked by Scripture. But how it is to happen is a shock. One of the Twelve will turn traitor to the Son of Man.

Tonight the set purpose of the Father will cross paths with the promptings of an evil heart. The Father's predetermined plan will join ranks with the premeditated kiss of Judas and lead the Passover Lamb to the slaughter. But before the angel of death comes to the cross, Jesus must eat the Passover meal with his disciples, Judas included.

While still outside of Jerusalem, Jesus orders two of his disciples to go ahead into the city. When they go, they find, just as Jesus had said, a certain man who was more than willing to provide his house for the Feast. Once the room is secured, the two make all of the preparations for the Passover meal. They take a spotless lamb to the temple to be sacrificed by the priest. On their way back, they purchase bread, bitter herbs, and wine. They roast the lamb and set the table. By evening, everything is ready for the Master.

As the sun sets, Jesus arrives with the rest of the disciples. The Twelve take their places around the table and Jesus sits down last, next to Judas. He treats Judas as his brother even though he knows that, after the bread has been broken and the cup has been passed, Judas will get up from the table of fellowship and leave the family of God forever. Soon he'll run away from the embrace of his Master and run toward the open arms of the conspirators, straight into the Devil's clasp.

Betrayal is always an inside job. It can only come at the hand of a friend. This foreknowledge pains Jesus. Such treachery is anticipated among enemies. But when the attack comes from within the ranks, at close range, it's unbearable—grief upon grief.

Beyond the murderous depths of the deed is the reality that Judas' chosen path will lead to two deaths: the Son of Man's as well as Judas'. Jesus is overwhelmed with sorrow. As its weight tries to crush the life out of him, he turns to his disciples during the meal, silences their table talk, and says,

> *"I have something hard but important to say to you: One of you is going to hand me over to the conspirators."*

> *They were stunned, and then began to ask, one after another, "It isn't me, is it, Master?"*

> *Jesus answered, "The one who hands me over is someone I eat with daily, one who passes me food at the table. In one sense the Son of Man is entering into a way of treachery well-marked by the Scriptures—no surprises here. In another sense that man who turns him in, turns traitor to the Son of Man—better never to have been born than do this!"* [1]

The disciples are stunned by this revelation. At first, the shock of such a statement numbs them. But then fear mixes with confusion and the two begin to pulse rapidly through their bodies. Still dazed, each of them begins to ask Jesus if he's the one who will turn traitor. Playing the charade, Judas turns to Jesus and asks with a straight face,

"It isn't me, is it, Rabbi?"

Jesus said, "Don't play games with me, Judas." [2]

Then he dipped the crust and gave it to Judas, son of Simon the Iscariot. As soon as the bread was in his hand, Satan entered him.

"What you must do," said Jesus, "do. Do it and get it over with." [3]

No more pretenses. No more masquerade. It's time for the real Judas to take off his mask and reveal his true intentions. Whatever he has purposed in his heart to do, Jesus tells him to do quickly. Eternity has been waiting for this moment. The cross is ready. Salvation is near. The appointed time has come. The Son of Man and the son of perdition must both play their parts.

With the thirty pieces of silver clanking in his purse, Judas leaves the Master's table. He now belongs to another—Satan. He has become hell's agent not by divine destiny but by his own rebellion. So dreadful is his decision that it would have been better if he hadn't been born.

While Jesus leaves the house and goes to the Garden of Gethsemane, Judas heads for the chief priests. He's going to make good on the blood money advanced to him. He'll lead them to the Son of Man, as promised, and deliver him with a prearranged signal. One last time he'll mask his deceit and betray his Master with a serpent's kiss.

> *"The one I kiss, that's the one—seize him." He went straight to Jesus, greeted him, "How are you, Rabbi?" and kissed him.* [4]

Reflection

When was the last time Jesus stunned you by saying something hard but important?

What does it feel like to be betrayed? Why is it that only a friend can betray a friend?

In what ways have you sold Jesus out? What was your price?

Is there any deceit in your relationship with Christ? In what ways has Jesus said to you: *"Don't play games with me."*?

Prayer

Father,

I wear many masks in my relationship with your Son. I masquerade as one of his followers and yet—too many times—my heart is far from him. There have been times when I have sold him out for far less than thirty pieces of silver. Like Judas, I have kissed his face only to stab him in the back.

During this day, don't let me go the way of Judas. Soften my heart. Break my will. Do whatever you need to do to save me from myself. When I am bent on betrayal, may your Son stun me with his grace. Even when I am about to turn him over with a kiss, may he still call me "friend". Assure me that the road to perdition is not divinely destined but rather paved by the steps of human rebellion. Remind me that the offer of eternal fellowship at your table comes to me through the sacrifice of your Son. Today, as I reflect on the sacrifice of Christ, may I receive his kiss from the cross. It's in Jesus' name I pray.

Amen.

[1]Matthew 26:21-24 [2]Matthew 26:25 [3]John 13:26-27 [4]Matthew 26:48-50

He Knows My Denial

Scripture Reading: Mark 14:27-31,66-72

Meditation

Tonight, Satan's on the prowl and he's salivating at the thought of a double portion—the Shepherd and his flock. Everyone knows that, once the Shepherd is gone, the sheep are easy prey. Attack Jesus and his disciples will scatter.

> *"I will strike the shepherd;*
> *The sheep will go helter-skelter."* [1]

But as Satan stalks, Jesus prays. While Jesus walks with his disciples toward the Mount of Olives, he warns them that their world is about to fall apart. In a few hours, their Messianic dreams will turn into a nightmare. Unthinkable fears will be realized; unimaginable pain will be endured.

The disciples' hopes will be shattered, scattered into too many fragments to piece back together. In the days to come, their faith will grope around in the darkness, desperately seeking something to grasp but finding nothing to hold. In the past, the disciples had stood by Jesus during his greatest trials. But in the attack that is about to come, they will all desert him. The coming days will bring times of tribulation unlike any the disciples have ever seen—unbearable to speak of, even more unbearable to pass through.

Soon, a pack of wolves, led by Judas, will come out to the Garden. When they bare their teeth and encircle Jesus, every one of the disciples will turn tail and run. They will forsake the Shepherd and save their own skin. None will remain. No one will stand by Jesus. No one will speak up. Instead, they will deny that they ever knew him.

On the way, Jesus tries to warn his disciples, especially Simon Peter.

> *"Simon, stay on your toes. Satan has tried his best to separate all of you from me, like chaff from wheat. Simon, I've prayed for you in particular that you not give in or give out. When you have come through the time of testing, turn to your companions and give them a fresh start."* [2]

These words are difficult for Simon Peter to hear. Throughout Jesus' ministry, he's been the most outspoken of the flock. When Jesus had asked the disciples their opinion about who he was, it was Simon who stood up and insisted that Jesus was the Messiah, the very Son of the living God.

Peter's confession and conviction are rock solid. He's passionate about following Christ, confident in his own leadership, and adamant about his faithfulness. Peter is insistent, to the point of making cutting comparisons to the rest of the disciples. He claims that he is both ready and willing to die for his Master.

> *"Even if everyone else is ashamed of you when things fall to pieces, I won't be."* [3]

Simon Peter bellows big words but they are words inflated with pride. They are filled with the air of self and not the spirit of faith. Just before they arrive at the Garden, Jesus deflates Peter's boasting by piercing it with a pointed prediction of defection.

> *"Don't be so sure. Today, this very night in fact, before the rooster crows twice, you will deny me three times."* [4]

Jesus' words are sharp and they are meant to puncture Peter's pride. His denial is not only certain; it's close. Imminent. No matter what Peter says, Jesus knows that it will happen. He is so sure of the event that he gives Peter the time, manner, frequency, and sign: tonight, a public disavowing, three times a denial, two times a rooster will crow. Peter breathes deep, puffs his chest out, and shouts back in protest,

"Even if I have to die with you, I will never deny you."
All the others said the same thing. 5

When Jesus arrives at the Garden of Gethsemane, the back-and-forth talk with Simon ends and prayer with his Father begins. After hours of great agony of soul, Jesus accepts the cup of suffering. He walks the way of the Father and goes out to meet his betrayer. As Judas approaches, Jesus bares his neck to the jaws of his enemy. Judas identifies him with a kiss. The soldiers bind him, strike him, and—as predicted—the flock scatters.

In the early morning hours, while the Jewish Ruling Council tries Jesus, Peter makes his way to the courtyard of the Chief Priest. While the religious leaders are inside, looking for a way to make the death penalty stick to Jesus, Peter mingles with the servants outside, warming himself by the fire. Love has brought him near but fear keeps him at a safe distance.

In the glow of the fire, a servant girl recognizes Peter. She points him out to the rest as a Christ follower but Peter denies it. Afraid of being outed as a follower of Christ, Peter leaves the fire and goes out onto the porch. As if on cue, a rooster crows. A few moments later, the servant girl spots Peter in the archway and insists, to his face, that he is one of the disciples. Once again, Peter denies it. After a little while, those gathered around the fire bring it up one more time.

"You've got to be one of them. You've got 'Galilean' written all over you."

Now Peter got really nervous and swore, "I never laid eyes on this man you're talking about." Just then the rooster crowed a second time. Peter remembered how Jesus had said, "Before a rooster crows twice, you'll deny me three times." [6]

As the rooster crows the second time, Jesus' prediction and Peter's betrayal meet. Fear has raised its voice and has silenced love. No longer proud or standing tall, Peter collapses in tears. But in the tears, Peter holds on to the words of Jesus,

"But after I am raised up, I will go ahead of you, leading the way to Galilee." [7]

"When you have come through the time of testing, turn to your companions and give them a fresh start." [8]

Jesus' prayer will have its way. Though the Shepherd is struck and the sheep are scattered, there will be a reunion. After the time of testing, death will be conquered, fear will be silenced, and Peter's love will be given voice once again.

Reflection

What bold and boastful statements have you made about your fidelity to Jesus?

In what ways have you been overcome by fear and denied any association with Christ?

When was the last time you felt like your world was falling to pieces and that you were left as a sheep without a Shepherd?

In what ways do you need Jesus to intercede for you against the schemes of Satan?

Prayer

Father,

I have made boastful statements about my fidelity to your Son. I have set up scenarios in my mind and bragged about the things that I would do or say. In my pride, I have compared myself to others, placing my actions on a higher pedestal. But when the time of testing comes, I often find myself like Peter: deserting the Christ; denying any association with him; defending myself; giving in to fear and finding my faith giving out. I am weeping many tears.

During this day, remind me that your Son lives to intercede for me. Assure me that, though my world might be falling to pieces, the plans of the Savior aren't falling apart. When I stray, comfort me with the promise that the Shepherd will search for me—none of the flock will be lost. Like Peter, when I go through the time of testing and fail, restore me with grace so that I might turn to my companions and give them a fresh start. In the name of Jesus I pray.

Amen.

[1]Mark 14:27 [2]Luke 22:31-32 [3]Mark 14:29 [4]Mark 14:30 [5]Mark 14:31
[6]Mark 14:70-72 [7]Mark 14:28 [8]Luke 22:32

Day 32:

He Knows My Remorse

Scripture Reading: Matthew 26:59-68; 27:1-10

Meditation

The traitorous deed is done. The transaction between Judas and the high priests is complete. The Son of Man is now in the hands of sinful men for the bargain price of thirty pieces of silver, compensation equivalent to that of a slave accidentally gored by an ox. Once again, the words that the prophet spoke about the Shepherd of Israel in days gone by have come alive in Jesus' time.

> *"Pay me what you think I'm worth." They paid me an insulting sum, counting out thirty silver coins.* [1]

After the religious leaders have Jesus in hand, they take him to stand trial before the Sanhedrin—the ruling religious body of the Jews. Throughout the night, one false witness after another steps up and presents bogus accusations and cooked up charges against Jesus.

Nothing sticks until the Chief Priest asks Jesus whether he is the Messiah. When Jesus claims to be the Messiah, the Chief Priest loses his temper, tears his robes, and starts yelling,

> *"He blasphemed! Why do we need witnesses to accuse him? You all heard him blaspheme! Are you going to stand for such blasphemy?"*

> *They all said, "Death! That seals his death sentence."* [2]

Blasphemy is the charge,
  "guilty" the verdict,
    and death the penalty.

When Judas learns of the sentence, he is overcome with remorse. He suddenly realizes that, for a handful of silver coins, he has delivered his Master—the Messiah—to the devil's agents on a silver platter. He has even sealed the deal with a kiss.

Though he tries to run from the accusations of his thoughts, he can't escape the damning testimony of his own heart; Jesus is doomed because of what he has done. And unless he does something to redeem himself, Judas fears that his own doom will soon follow. For the first time since the blood money changed hands, he's having second thoughts.

> *"Oh no! What have I done? I've betrayed an innocent man. His blood is going to be on my hands. He's doomed. And so am I."*

The coins that clink in Judas' purse rattle his soul. Attached to the thirty pieces of silver is a costly consequence—terror of conscience and torment of soul. This is more than he had bargained for.

The one turned traitor has just been snake bitten. Little did Judas know that the serpent of betrayal always strikes twice. First it bites the one who is betrayed and then it recoils on the hand that holds it.

The venom of betrayal is quickly moving towards Judas' soul and, if the poison isn't removed soon, death is imminent. Sorrow over his sin has put a salve on the bite but only forgiveness will remove the poison.

Driven by remorse, Judas goes looking for redemption. But he goes looking for it in the wrong place. He doesn't run to Jesus. He runs to the brood of vipers, the high priests. But they don't care about the terror of a soul. Worse than that, they can't give what they don't have. They're spiritually bankrupt themselves.

But Judas is determined to buy back his soul from the high priests. Like a dog returning to its vomit, he runs to the Temple, holds out the thirty pieces of silver to the high priests, bares his heart, and begs for redemption.

"I've sinned. I've betrayed an innocent man." [3]

As Judas bids for forgiveness, the high priests turn their heads at his offer.

"What do we care? That's your problem!" [4]

Redemption can't be found at the hands of the high priests. Their policy is no refunds on blood money. What's bought can't be returned. Though Judas' confession is sincere, forgiveness isn't for sale. No amount of money can buy back the kiss in the Garden. When it comes to betrayal, all sales are final.

Locked out of the kingdom of grace, Judas' remorse turns into despair. He sees no way out, nowhere to turn, and no one else to run to. Without forgiveness, he can't bear to live with what he has done. His body is alive but his spirit is dying from a lack of grace. Spiritually busted, Judas decides to cash out. He throws the blood money across the Temple floor, runs out to the nearest hill, finds a tree, and begins to form a noose.

While Judas is bent on taking his life, Jesus, his Master, is ready and determined to give his life as a ransom for many. Soon Judas and Jesus will each hang from a tree. One will hang from a noose; the other will stand tall and hold fast to the nails. Despair, coupled with the belief that there is no other way, will take one life; love, married to the belief that this is the Father's way, will offer up the other.

Though both trees will bear the penalty of sin, only one will pay the price for redemption. From the cross, Jesus will say the words that Judas longs to hear,

> *"Father, forgive them; they don't know what they're doing."* [5]

Such redemption can't be bought with gold or silver. It doesn't come from the hands of bankrupt men. It can only be given, free and clear, from the hands of a Savior who is rich in grace and generous in mercy

Reflection

Have you ever been overcome with remorse because of your sin?

Like Judas, how have you tried to purchase your own redemption? Why is Christ's payment the only redemption for sin?

When Judas ran to the chief priests and confessed his sin, they said, *"What do we care? That's your problem!"*

Why do all efforts at self-redemption lead to death?

How does Christ respond to a sinner's plea?

Prayer

Father,

Like Judas, I have a price by which my loyalty to Christ can be bought. In many ways and at many times I have sold out your Son. But as the silver coins clink in my pocket, my soul rattles with remorse. I am suffering terror of conscience and torment of soul and these are more than I have bargained for. In many ways, I have tried to atone for my sins but have found that redemption is not for sale.

During this day, create faith in me to believe that the cross is the only place I need to run. Remind me that forgiveness can't be bought with such perishable things as gold or silver but only with the precious blood of your Son, Jesus Christ. When my remorse turns to despair, lead me away from the tree of destruction and bring me to the tree of life. As I gaze upon the crucified Christ, let me hear the only words that give life,

> *"Father, forgive them; they don't know what they're doing."*

It's in your Son's name that I pray.

Amen.

[1]Zechariah 11:12 [2]Matthew 26:65-66 [3]Matthew 27:4 [4]Matthew 27:4 [5]Luke 23:34

Day 33:

He Knows My Neutrality

Scripture Reading: Matthew 27:11-26

Meditation

Pontius Pilate is a good politician.

As prefect of the Judean province, he knows whom to please and how best to please them. In his tenure, he has learned that the best political decisions aren't always the morally right ones but the ones most expedient. Pilate commits only when he needs to commit. He plays the center when the costs are too high on either side. He only fights the battles that he can win and sits out the rest. And, above all else, he makes certain that he saves face before Caesar.

When it comes to the interest of Tiberius Caesar, Pilate rules the turbulent province of Judea with a heavy hand. Tiberius has appointed Pilate to keep the peace and his Caesar's expectation is that there be nothing less than law and order. The Pax Romana must not be disturbed. It would be best if the sleeping dogs of Rome were left to lie.

But the land of the Jews is filled with rebellious children. The descendants of Abraham, Isaac, and Jacob are a fiercely nationalistic people. They are headstrong toward any authority that tries to put them under rule and prone to public temper tantrums in order to get their way.

After years of Roman rule, the children of Israel have figured out that Pilate responds best to large crowds, noisy delegations, and the threat to riot.

Fueling their insurrectionist zeal is the promise of a Messiah-King. And these days it has been stoked by the belief that he is coming soon.

The Jews believe that when this Messiah-King comes, he will conquer and cast out the infidel. He will physically restore the kingdom of glory to Israel, set up the royal throne of his father David, and reign forever. The rod of Rome will be broken and the Shepherd of Israel will lead his sheep to quiet waters.

During his rule, Pilate has learned a thing or two about the sons of Israel. He knows that they're really no threat to the iron fist of Rome, but they are an irritant. Trying to put your hands around them is like grabbing hold of a splintered limb; grab too tight and you'll get your share of slivers. When dealing with the tree of David, Pilate has decided that it's best either to strike the limb with an ax or to keep your hands off. Knowing when to do which is Pilate's constant dilemma.

To Pilate's credit, he's made some progress in the region. His men have just captured the infamous insurrectionist, Jesus Barabbas. Soon this nationalistic hero of Zion will hang from a cross as a warning and example to all who pass by: resist Rome and you'll get nailed to a tree.

When it comes to slithering through the political process, the Jewish Council is as shrewd as a serpent. Its members know that Pilate cares nothing about the religious matters of the Jews. In order to procure the death sentence against Jesus, they'll need more than the theological charge of blasphemy; they'll need a political charge—treason.

As they bring Jesus to Pilate, they charge the Prince of Peace with disturbing the peace of Rome.

"We found this man undermining our law and order, forbidding taxes to be paid to Caesar, setting himself up as Messiah-King." [1]

Pilate's ears perk.

Treason is a serious accusation and so Pilate takes a hands on approach. The governor is intent on hearing the case but he's also leery of the religious leaders' motive. He knows the Jews all too well. He wonders why a people so bent on nationalistic liberty and so vehement against Rome would voluntarily turn in an enemy of the state.

It doesn't take Pilate long to figure out the game. The Jewish Ruling Council is trying to play him like a pawn. They want Jesus dead. And in order for that to happen, they need him to turn his thumb down on this lowly Jew and send him to the cross. Pilate sees the motive behind the charge—spite for Christ, not loyalty to Caesar.

But after Pilate questions Jesus, he sees no threat to Rome and no basis for crucifixion. Always playing the role of the politician, he offers the Jews an alternative judgment.

In keeping with an old Passover custom, Pilate offers to pardon a prisoner named by the crowd. He gives them two choices:

"Jesus Barabbas or Jesus the so-called Christ?"

The crowd, spurred on by the Jewish Ruling Council, shouts for Barabbas. Trying to reconcile the truth deposited in his conscience with the vehement consensus of the people, Pilate asks,

> *"Then what do I do with Jesus, the so-called Christ?"*
>
> *They all shouted, "Nail him to a cross!"*
>
> *He objected, "But for what crime?"*
>
> *But they yelled all the louder, "Nail him to a cross!"* [2]

Warned by his wife not to get mixed up in judging Jesus and seeing that the crowd might soon riot, Pilate makes the political choice—neutrality, hands off of Jesus. The costs are too high on either side. Best to walk the middle road.

Wanting to declare himself innocent of Jesus' blood, Pilate asks for a bowl of water. As he stands before the crowd, he performs a Jewish purification ritual as prescribed by the Mosaic Law.

> *Finally, all the leaders of that town that is nearest the body will wash their hands over the heifer that had its neck broken at the stream and say, "We didn't kill this man and we didn't see who did it. Purify your people Israel whom you redeemed, O God. Clear your people Israel from any guilt in this murder."* [3]

As Jesus goes to the cross, the reign of the Messiah-King begins. From the nail pierced hands of the Prince of Peace there will be no posture of neutrality; all have sinned but the sacrifice of Christ is all-sufficient. Rome may remain for a time but the kingdom of grace will rule.

Reflection

Why is it impossible to stay neutral when it comes to Jesus the Christ?

What type of rioting mob is there in your world? In what ways have you been intimidated by the mob and washed your hands of Christ?

If you were to take a stand for Christ, what could you lose? What could you gain?

What comfort does it bring to you to know that Christ has no posture of neutrality towards you?

Prayer

Father,

I confess that, when the crowd has threatened me, I have taken a neutral stand concerning your Son. I have gone against my conscience and have chosen to walk the road of diplomacy. To ease my sense of accountability, I have washed my hands of any responsibility for the King of the Jews. I have handed him over to the mob to do with as they wish. In washing my hands, I have soiled my soul.

During this day, give me the courage of your Holy Spirit so that I might stand up against the crowd and take a stand for Christ. Help me see through the false charges of the mob to the real motive—spite for the Son of God. When I fear that the blood of Christ is on my hands, drive me to the sacrifice of the cross. As I gaze at the King of the Jews, assure me that though his blood may be on my hands, it is a blood that will cleanse me and make me whiter than snow. Remind me that, with the Prince of Peace, there is no posture of neutrality; all have sinned but his sacrifice is all-sufficient. It's in Jesus' name that I pray.

Amen.

[1]Luke 23:2 [2]Matthew 27:22-23 [3]Deuteronomy 21:6-8

Day 34:

He Knows My Insults

Scripture Reading: Mark 15:16-32

Meditation

Throughout the Passion of the Christ, insult upon insult is added to injury.

During it all, Jesus stands silent. He's like a lamb about to be taken to the slaughter. There is no response to the accusations. No words spoken in self-defense. Only silence. It's the mark of Isaiah's Suffering Servant.

> *"He was beaten, he was tortured,*
> *but he didn't say a word.*
> *Like a lamb taken to be slaughtered*
> *and like a sheep being sheared,*
> *he took it all in silence.*
> *Justice miscarried, and he was led off—*
> *and did anyone really know what*
> *was happening?"* [1]

As Jesus stands before Pilate, justice miscarries. Hope for the Son of Man lies stillborn in the ceremonially washed hands of a politician who cares more about his position before Caesar than his responsibility to the Messiah-King. His decision concerning Jesus is to make no decision. Persuaded by his wife's dream and pressured by the threats of the crowd, Pilate aborts the truth that has been conceived in his heart. He grabs the basin, and as the water flows, he symbolically rids himself of any guilt for the blood of the King of the Jews. From a posture of neutrality, he acquiesces to the will of the Jewish Ruling Council. He gives the murderous mob what they want—the King of the Jews, crucified on a cross.

A Jew claiming to be a King is an easy target for a company of Roman soldiers with plenty of time to kill and nothing to kill it with. Jesus is a welcomed whipping boy.

To the scourging, the soldiers add a little sport. They find a purple robe, fashion a crown of thorns from a nearby bush, and begin to ape worship, mimicking regard reserved only for Caesar.

"Bravo, King of the Jews!" 2

As they repeatedly strike, spit, and mock Jesus, the King of the Jews remains silent.

After the soldiers have had their fun, they take off the purple robe and march Jesus out to Golgotha—"Skull Hill"—to crucify him. Along the way, they offer him wine mixed with myrrh, a mild analgesic to numb the pain. Jesus refuses to accept it. The Son of Man wants his senses fully intact during the crucifixion. As the sin substitute, he needs to feel the full anger of men and experience the full wrath of God. There will be no deadening of the pain. Every blow of the hammer must be felt. Every insult will be heard. He will die fully aware, fully alert.

When they reach Golgotha, the soldiers strip Jesus of his clothes and crucify him between two criminals. Crucifixion is a Roman death penalty that nails the condemned on two beams—excruciating pain and humiliation. It's a form of execution created to strip a man of his dignity, expose his sin, and leave him vulnerable to the derision of all who pass by.

As Jesus hangs, the prophetic words of David become history,

> *"And here I am, a nothing—an earthworm,*
> *something to step on, to squash.*
> *Everyone pokes fun at me;*
> *they make faces at me, they shake their heads:*
> *'Let's see how God handles this one;*
> *since God likes him so much, let him help him!' "* [3]

The only weapon that the crucified have are the two edged swords of their tongues. Their pleas for mercy have long ceased. Only curses for those around the cross remain. If not curses, then at least rebuke. But while the criminals hanging next to him curse the crowd, Jesus remains silent.

As people walk the thoroughfare that leads in and out of Jerusalem, they shake their heads in disgust at those hanging on the cross. Remembering Jesus' words about the Temple, some begin to taunt him, daring him to come down from the cross.

> *"You bragged that you could tear down the Temple and then rebuild it in three days—so show us your stuff! Save yourself! If you're really God's Son, come down from that cross!"* [4]

They are unaware that the Temple that they speak of is Jesus and it is being destroyed. The blow of the executioner's hammer has shaken the foundation. Every insult from the crowd pushes over one of the remaining columns. Soon death will come and sweep the rubble that once housed the Holy of Holies away. But on the third day, Jesus said the Temple would be rebuilt. He would rise again and the Word made flesh would tabernacle with his people forever. But for now, the Word is silent.

The high priests and religion scholars are also at the cross. They're the ones in the middle of the crowd, mixing it up, laughing as they poke fun at Jesus.

> *"He saved others—but he can't save himself! Messiah, is he? King of Israel? Then let him climb down from that cross. We'll all become believers then!"* 5

Even the two criminals that are crucified next to Christ pile on the insults.

> *"Some Messiah you are! Save yourself! Save us!"* 6

Through it all, Jesus holds his tongue. He keeps the blade of his rebuke sheathed. As he hangs, there is no threat of retaliation. No revenge or reproof. In silence he takes the full punishment of sin and, in return, bestows grace speaking louder than words.

Reflection

How have you, out of ignorance or spite, insulted the Son of God?

In what way is the silence of Christ on the cross a gift of grace?

Why was it important for Jesus to refuse the painkiller and experience the full force of the crucifixion?

When the crowd taunted Jesus to save himself and come down from the cross, he clung to the nails. What are the redemptive consequences of that decision?

Prayer

Father,

I confess that I have insulted the Son of Man in many and various ways. Like Pilate, I have chosen to do nothing instead of something. Like the soldiers, I have aped worship and mocked the kingship of the Messiah. Like those passing by the cross, I have challenged the Christ to prove himself to be the Son of God, taunting him to do the miraculous. Like those crucified with your Son, I have accused the Messiah of being too impotent to help and too callous to care.

During this day, help me rejoice in the silence of your Son. Show me that heaven's grace is spoken in the hush of the cross. No words spoken in retaliation. No revenge. Only redemption. As your Son held his tongue, not condemning those for the great offense of their mouths, may he also, this day, grab hold of my tongue. As I stand before the cross, may he replace my insults with words of praise and fill my mouth with shouts of joy. In the name of Christ I pray.

Amen.

[1]Isaiah 53:7-8 [2]Mark 15:18 [3]Psalm 22:6-8 [4]Mark 15:29-30 [5]Mark 15:31-32 [6]Luke 23:39

The Shelter of Love

"Your beauty and love chase
after me every day of my life."
Psalm 23:6a

As the Good Shepherd leads the flock toward home, his beauty and love, like two tireless sheepdogs, bring up the rear. Every day they work the fields and watch over the flock. No need to fear what is behind, or what is on either side.

Beauty and love are pursuers, quick to pick up the scent of a beloved stray and even quicker to track it down. When the sheep begin to wander aimlessly, beauty chases down one flank and love the other. The two keep the flock together. Safety is in the fold. They guard the rear and watch the flanks, always quick to intervene.

As you move toward the end of your forty days with Christ, reflect on the following ...

Reflection

When was the last time that you strayed away from the flock?

In what ways has the beauty and love of Christ chased after you?

How is Christ pursuing you every day of your life?

Day 35:
He Knows My
Eleventh Hour Request

Scripture Reading: Luke 23:32-43

Meditation

In death, as in life, Jesus keeps company with sinners.

Since his ministry began, the religious leaders have accused Jesus of hanging around the riffraff. When he talked about the value of lost things, the religious leaders were right there, watching with a legalistic eye, pointing their fingers, and shaking their heads in disgust.

> *By this time a lot of men and women of doubtful reputation were hanging around Jesus, listening intently. The Pharisees and religion scholars were not pleased, not at all pleased. They growled, "He takes in sinners and eats meals with them, treating them like old friends."* [1]

Finally, in these last days, the religious leaders have found a way to condemn Jesus for the company he keeps. His crucifixion between the two criminals is meant to signify guilt by association to all who pass by. Jesus shares the penalty for sin, but unlike the two men he hangs with, he's innocent of the crime.

Sinner? *No!*

Friend of sinners? *Yes!*

For the two criminals crucified next to Jesus, these are the final minutes of the eleventh hour. Death is near. Strength to push the legs up and chest out in order to fill the lungs with air is fading. Every breath is a hard fought prize. As the final grains of sand stream through the hourglass, their words are few and measured. One of the criminals wastes his breath by damning the soldiers below for nailing him to the cross. Catching his breath, he turns his head to Jesus and curses him for keeping him on the cross. The coming specter of death has hardened his heart.

"Some Messiah you are! Save yourself! Save us!" [2]

But when the other criminal hears the curses that are hurled at Jesus, he gathers whatever strength he has left and begins to rebuke his partner in crime.

"Have you no fear of God? You're getting the same as him. We deserve this, but not him—he did nothing to deserve this." [3]

This criminal understands the penalty of justice. He's getting what he deserves and so is his partner. But Jesus is innocent.

As the criminal defends the Son of Man, he, a dying man, is born again. A few hours ago, he had mimicked the insults of his partner. From the opposite side of the cross, he had shouted the same cutting words into Jesus' other ear. The nails had made his heart callous and cold, ready for the coffin. But when he heard Jesus ask his Father to forgive the ones who were crucifying him, his heart of stone crumbled. A new heart was given—and with it—a new spirit and the hope for new life.

Believing that he has nothing to lose and everything to gain, he turns toward Jesus and, with words broken by shallow breaths, he pleads,

"Jesus, remember me when you enter your kingdom." [4]

The request is audacious. The criminal is asking that the verdict of justice that nailed him to the cross be overridden by the grace of Christ. Though he deserves death and Hades, he pleads for that which he doesn't deserve—Paradise.

Jesus hears the beat of a new heart and makes it skip. To an eleventh hour plea he gives an eternal promise.

"Don't worry, I will. Today you will join me in paradise." [5]

Jesus assures this new child of God that, though death may come, his life won't end. Today it will continue in Paradise.

The fullness of the promise means that, when the final grain of sand falls in the hourglass, the criminal will leave his partner in crime hanging on the cross and walk hand in hand with Christ, the second Adam, into the splendor of the new Eden. When the criminal breathes his last breath, his today will turn into a never ending tomorrow. And when his eyes open, he will be in a different place, a better place, the place of Christ, forever.

A place filled with exuberance and laughter,
thankful voices and melodic songs. [6]

Just like the father who welcomed the prodigal son home, from the cross Jesus opens wide the doors of heaven. He clothes the naked criminal with the robe of his righteousness. He gives him sandals to walk in the Garden of God. He puts the family ring on his finger, calls for a feast, and then invites all of the angels of heaven to come and celebrate.

*"Quick. Bring a clean set of clothes and dress him.
Put the family ring on his finger and sandals on his feet.
Then get a grain-fed heifer and roast it. We're going to
feast! We're going to have a wonderful time! My son is
here—given up for dead and now alive! Given up for
lost and now found!" And they began to have a wonderful time.* 7

In death, as in life, Jesus keeps company with sinners. In
Christ, eleventh hour requests are never too late. They're
given eternal responses.

Reflection

The religious leaders accused Jesus of hanging around the riffraff. What comfort is there in knowing that the Savior treated sinners like old friends?

What's the significance of Christ being crucified between two criminals?

What would your eleventh hour request be?

How is Christ's promise of Paradise your possession?

Prayer

Father,

Like the criminal on the cross, I am guilty and deserve nothing but the hammer of justice to nail me to the cross. In the suffering brought on by my sin, I have insulted your Son. I have mocked his sacrifice, accused him of being too callous to care, and too weak to act on my behalf. As death approaches, my heart has become as hard as stone.

During this day, let me hear your Son's words of forgiveness. Through those words shatter my heart of stone and give me a new heart: a heart that dares to ask for that which it doesn't deserve—Paradise. Assure me that in and because of the sacrifice of your Son, the answer to my eleventh hour request is "yes." Comfort me with the fact that, when I breathe my last in this life, I will open my eyes and see Christ face to face, forever. I pray this in the name of him who treats sinners like old friends.

Amen

[1]Luke 15:1-2 [2]Luke 23:39 [3]Luke 23:40 [4]Luke 23:42 [5]Luke 23:43 [6]Isaiah 51:3 [7]Luke 15:22-24

Day 36:
He Knows My Grief

Scripture Reading: Luke 23:44–24:12

Meditation

The events of the past few days have struck a violent blow to the heart of the women who have followed Jesus from Galilee. Just last week, all of Jerusalem's people had hailed their Master as a king but today they nailed him to a tree like a criminal.

As Mary Magdalene, Joanna, Mary, the mother of James, and the other women gather around the cross, they are still in a state of shock. Their Master's crucifixion is so violent that their emotions haven't been able to keep pace with the horror of the cross. Shock, denial, and anger have all been stopping points along the way. As Jesus struggles for his last breaths, their emotions are beginning to catch up to the bitter reality of the moment.

Jesus is dying. Death is on its way.

Knowing that heaven's redemptive work is now finished here on earth, Jesus commits his spirit into his Father's hands. He bows his head and breathes his last. Death, eager to claim its prize, comes riding towards Skull Hill on a pale horse. As he gallops past the cross, he unsheathes and swings a two-edged sword. With a downward swing, the blade cuts short the life of the Son of Man; on its upward return, it slashes deeply into the hearts of the beloved women who keep vigil around the cross.

Death's blade has dealt the women more than a flesh wound; it has sliced through their flesh and bone and punctured the very depths of their being—heart, spirit, strength, and mind. Finality is the razor sharp point that pierces their souls. Death has silenced the gentle sound of their Master's voice. It has shut his eyes. Stilled his hands. There will be no more gentle words for fragile and frail lives. No glance of grace that stills the soul. No tender touch.

Burial is the last sting of death. Death steals away the one loved but burial seals the loved one away, forever. When the tomb is closed, then, all is lost.

As Joseph of Arimathea takes Jesus' body down from the cross and carries it to the tomb, the women are overwhelmed by sorrow. Unthinkable pain mixes with their tears and inexpressible grief begins to bleed out. All the ties holding their world together have now been severed from their anchor point. The women have been cut loose from all that they hold dear and now they have nothing to cling to except their grief. And grief holding on to grief begets only more grief.

Grief is a cruel jailer. As the tomb is sealed, the women are imprisoned in the pain of the present moment. Mourning shackles their memory; it refuses to open the door of remembrance. Though Jesus had written many resurrection words on their hearts, the flood of their tears has smeared the ink of his promise. Sobs of sorrow have blurred his words, making the promises hard to decipher and even more difficult to remember.

As the women leave the tomb, all they carry with them is grief. They have no resurrection expectations. No thoughts of yesterday. No hopes for tomorrow. They are buried in the pain of the now.

That all of these things happened to their Master should have come as no surprise to the women. Three times during his ministry Jesus had predicted the specific details of his Passion: handed over to the Romans in Jerusalem, condemned to die, killed, but on the third day alive again.

> *"Listen carefully. We're on our way up to Jerusalem.*
> *Everything written in the Prophets about the Son of Man*
> *will take place. He will be handed over to the Romans,*
> *jeered at, made sport of, and spit on. Then, after giving*
> *him the third degree, they will kill him. In three days he*
> *will rise, alive." But they didn't get it, could make neither*
> *heads nor tails of what he was talking about.* [1]

That this was to happen—*undeniable.*
That it did happen—*unbearable.*
What would happen next—*unbelievable.*

Very early in the morning on the third day after his death, Jesus comes alive—just like he had promised.

When the women bring the spices to the tomb to finish preparing their Master's body for burial, they find the stone rolled away but his body has gone missing. Their memory, still numbed by grief, can't put the pieces together. They grope for logical answers: *grave robbers? the gardener moving the body? Rome and the religious leaders?* None of them dares to think about the possibility of a resurrection. Such hope died with their Master on Friday.

Suddenly two angels appear out of nowhere. The women are awestruck; as they tremble with fear, their knees buckle in worship.

The angels ask the women,

"Why are you looking for the Living One in a cemetery? He is not here, but raised up. Remember how he told you when you were still back in Galilee that he had to be handed over to sinners, be killed on a cross, and in three days rise up?" Then they remembered Jesus' words. [2]

For two days, grief had held a death grip on the women's hearts. But now, on the third day, angelic news pries fingers of sorrow loose. The messengers of God don't tell the women anything new; they only remind them of the things that they already know. The angels' proclamation simply unearths the treasure that the Savior had buried deep within the women's souls:

"The cross is necessary. Sin demands a payment. Death is the price. Death won't have the last word. The resurrection will follow. In death and in life, hold onto the Promise."

Reflection

Has grief ever numbed your memory to the promises of Christ?

In what areas of your life are you like the women who went to the tomb, confused, shaking your head, and puzzled at the work of God?

What would it be like to live without any resurrection expectations?

What promise is the Living One asking you to remember on this day?

Prayer

Father,

Like the women who witnessed your Son's crucifixion, grief has a death grip on my heart. Whenever it comes, it imprisons me in the pain of the present moment. Sorrow shackles me. Mourning blocks my memory to the promises of Christ. I am too weak to take comfort in the words of the past and too afraid to walk into the future.

During this day, loosen the grip that grief has on my life. Send messengers to point me to the resurrection of the Master and remind me that, though death does come, life will follow. Comfort me with the fact that, no matter the number of tears or the depth of sorrow, the promise of Christ always remains secure. Surprise me this day with good news from the graveyard. And seeing once again that the Savior's tomb is empty, may I walk—upright and resurrected—out of mine. In Jesus' name I pray.

Amen.

[1]Luke 18:31-34 [2]Luke 24:5-8

Day 37:
He Knows My
Slowness To Believe

Scripture Reading: Luke 24:13-35

Meditation

Emmaus is a small village only a brisk afternoon's walk out-side of Jerusalem. For two traveling together, the seven miles can be easily bridged by a steady gait spurred on by plenty of spirited conversation. But for a pair of Jesus' disciples burdened by unbelief, the road from Jerusalem to Emmaus has just stretched into a long walk, journeyed with even longer faces.

It's the third day after their Master's crucifixion and, as they walk, they carry heavy hearts. Just a week ago, they had marched with Jesus into Jerusalem. At that time, their steps were as high as their hopes. The crowd shouted "Hosannas" and the two disciples had every reason to believe that their Master was the promised Messiah, the One who would restore the kingdom of Israel.

But as the week progressed, everything turned on a heel. One from among them had betrayed Jesus. The religious lead-ers brought Jesus before Pilate, got him sentenced to death, and crucified him. When he was dead, a respected disciple, a member of the Jewish Ruling Council, asked Pilate for his body and buried him in a new tomb.

Adding confusion to the chaos was the fact that some of the women who had followed Jesus all the way from Galilee had gone to the tomb early in the morning. They saw the stone rolled away from the tomb but they couldn't find his body. Running back to the Eleven, they shouted a story about seeing angels who had said that Jesus was alive. But when the disciples pushed for proof, none of the women could say that they had actually seen Jesus.

As the two disciples walk the Emmaus road, the weight of their confusion shortens their stride. It slows their gait until the pace of their steps matches the beat of their faith: slow, plodding, trudging along. With each step, they're trying to put the pieces of the week together. They've heard the resurrection stories but no one has seen the resurrected Savior. Until they have a body they can touch, it's hard for them to believe that the Master is really alive. It's all such a mystery.

In the middle of their conversation, Jesus comes up and walks alongside them. Though he's an arm's length away from them, they don't recognize him. Overhearing the confusion in their conversation, he asks,

> *"What's this you're discussing so intently as you walk along?"*
>
> *They just stood there, long-faced, like they had lost their best friend. Then one of them, his name was Cleopas, said, "Are you the only one in Jerusalem who hasn't heard what's happened during the last few days?"*
>
> *He said, "What has happened?"* [1]

Cleopas and his traveling partner alternate words as they try to explain all of the things that had happened to their Master during the past week. In staccato fashion, they rattle off a concise summary of the Passion.

"Jesus. A man of God. A prophet. Mighty in work and word. Blessed by heaven and on earth. High hopes that he was the One. The Messiah. Deliverer of Israel. Hopes dashed. Betrayed by High Priests. Sentenced to death. Crucified. Buried. Third day. Tomb empty. But no body."

Jesus' response halts their feet and arrests their hearts,

"So thick-headed! So slow-hearted! Why can't you simply believe all that the prophets said? Don't you see that these things had to happen, that the Messiah had to suffer and only then enter into his glory?" [2]

The disciples are stunned by his words. Seeing the color run from their faces, Jesus fires their hearts with the spark of the Spirit. Ready to walk again, Jesus takes the lead and blazes the trail by walking them through all of the Christ Scriptures.

Then he started at the beginning, with the Books of Moses, and went on through all the Prophets, pointing out everything in the Scriptures that referred to him. [3]

With each Scripture that Jesus opens, the disciples' hearts burn and their steps quicken. Though they are moving, time seems to stand still.

Before they know it, they come to the edge of the village. Jesus acts as if he's going on further but they press him to stay the night. He agrees and goes in with them. As he sits down at the table, he plays the role of the host. He takes the bread, blesses it, breaks it and gives it to them. It's at that moment that their eyes are opened. But as soon as they recognize him, he disappears.

Excitedly they banter back and forth,

"Didn't we feel on fire as he conversed with us on the road, as he opened up the Scriptures for us?" [4]

Finally, the two disciples put all of the pieces together. Not wasting a minute, they run the seven miles back to Jerusalem—hearts ablaze, feet on fire. They find the Eleven and all of their friends and animatedly explain,

"It was him all along. Scripture opened—all of it's about him. The spark of the Spirit. Our hearts on fire. Faith beating fast. The breaking of bread. All of these things had to happen. It's really true. The Master is alive!"

Reflection

How are you thick-headed and slow-hearted to believe?

When was the last time you felt your heart on fire within you?

In what ways are you struggling to put all of the pieces about Christ together?

What is the central message of Scripture? Using only the Old Testament Scriptures, can you point to Christ?

Prayer

Father,

Like the two disciples walking the Emmaus Road, I am so thick-headed to understand and so slow-hearted to believe all that your Son has done for me. Step after step, I plod along in my spiritual walk. All too many days I am weighed down by doubt and hampered by a heavy heart. Though your Son has promised to walk with me all the days of my life, I am often blind to his presence and deaf to his voice.

During this day, set my heart on fire with the presence of Christ. As I walk throughout this day, open wide my eyes and loose my ears so that I might see and hear Christ along my way. Ignite my faith by the spark of the Spirit. Open the Scriptures and show me that all things point to your Son. After seeing Christ in the Word, set my feet ablaze and quicken my steps with the good news of the Gospel. May my message be that of the Emmaus' disciples: Jesus is the Christ—the one who was crucified, killed, and risen for the forgiveness of sins. It's in his name that I pray.

Amen

1Luke 24:17-19 2Luke 24:25-26 3Luke 24:27 4Luke 24:32

Day 38:
He Knows My Doubt

Scripture Reading: John 20:19-31

Meditation

The Evil One is the father of two fraternal twins: terror and doubt.

During the Passion of the Christ, Satan's demons dropped these two hellions on the doorstep of the disciples. When the disciples answered the door, the two unruly children pushed their way into the house of faith and began to wreak torment of soul and terror of conscience. Like defiant children, they destroyed the peace. And it's such peace, at this time, that the disciples need most.

The Jewish leaders have just struck the Good Shepherd dead. The blow has scattered the Messiah's little flock. Now the temple police, looking to put an end to this blasphemer's influence and to send a message to any who would want to continue his cause, are trying to round up the benumbed sheep and bring them to slaughter. The disciples have become fugitives on the lam.

Members of the little flock, vulnerable and frightened, have gathered together in a small room. As they huddle behind locked doors, they plan possible escape routes out of Jerusalem. They long for the safety of Galilean soil. They believe that familiar territory will ease the terror. If the place of the Passion is out of sight, then it's out of mind. Until they can make their getaway, they need to lay low, keep quiet, and throw the wolf off the trail of their scent. The word is spread throughout the flock: public movement must be kept to a minimum; travel only under the cover of darkness; keep the doors locked at all times. If anyone knocks at the door, first identify then unlock.

But when Jesus comes to the door he doesn't knock. In his post resurrection body, he walks directly through the door and enters the disciples' presence. Standing among the frightened flock, Jesus says the word they most long to hear,

"Peace to you." [1]

His words aren't empty well wishes; they are accompanied by his physical presence. He substantiates his message by showing them the nail prints in his hands and the spear wound in his side. These are the definitive marks of their Master. He's not a ghost or an apparition. He's the crucified Messiah, resurrected in the flesh. As soon as the disciples see the scars, the devil's twins—terror and doubt—exit the room. Heaven's children—peace and hope—take up residence.

But Thomas, one of the Twelve, sometimes called the Twin, isn't with the disciples. When he returns to the room where they are staying, the disciples excitedly and repeatedly tell him that they have just seen the Master. But the more the disciples insist, the more Thomas resists.

"Unless I see the nail holes in his hands, put my finger in the nail holes, and stick my hand in his side, I won't believe it." [2]

Thomas is a practical man, deliberate in his discipleship. He's the one among the Twelve who keeps his feet on the ground while the others get lifted away by fleeting, highflying emotions. He calculates the risks, counts the costs, and then, based on the facts, decides to invest his life in a certain cause. Once he commits, his loyalty is as good as gold. He's steady, as he demonstrated so ably when Jesus went to Judea to raise Lazarus from the dead. Even though some of the disciples had warned Jesus to stay put because the Jews were going all out to kill him, Thomas, thought it through and urged his peers,

"Come along. We might as well die with him." [3]

Thomas is no-nonsense but he also likes things to make sense. Before he moves, he likes to measure every step. He has a methodical, matter-of-fact way of assessing situations and solving problems. When Jesus talked about eternal rooms in the Father's house and the road that leads there, it was Thomas who asked the logical question that everyone else was thinking,

> *"Master, we have no idea where you're going. How do you expect us to know the road?"*
>
> *Jesus said, "I am the Road, also the Truth, also the Life. No one gets to the Father apart from me."* [4]

For Thomas, the pain of his Master's death is greater than the promise of the resurrection. Right now it's safer and easier for him to believe the worst than to dare to hope for the best. False hope is more painful than no hope. Without proof, Thomas chooses to hold onto his doubt. Right now he would rather cling to the pain than to risk reaching into the darkness for hope. Even the urging of his fellow disciples can't change his mind. His pain demands proof.

"Unless ..."

Eight days later, Thomas' conditional "unless" comes full circle. The disciples are again in the same room and this time Thomas is with them. Just as before, Jesus walks through locked doors. After calming them with his words of peace, Jesus turns his attention directly to Thomas. He gives no lecture. No upbraiding. He just reaches out his hands and offers an incarnational invitation to Thomas.

*"Take your finger and examine my hands. Take your
hand and stick it in my side. Don't be unbelieving.
Believe."* [5]

Before Thomas can reach for the scars, the pierced hand of
the Savior grabs his heart. Faith begins to beat fast. Hope now
has an object to which it can cling.

Thomas said, "My Master! My God!"

*Jesus said, "So, you believe because you've seen with
your own eyes. Even better blessings are in store for
those who believe without seeing."* [6]

Reflection

What doors are you locked behind? Who or what do you fear?

When was the last time you demanded proof before you would believe? Did you get it?

Thomas said, *"Unless I see the nail holes ... I won't believe it."* What's your "unless"?

Why is it safer to believe the worst than to dare to hope for the best?

Prayer

Father,

I so desire peace and yet terror and doubt torment me. Sometimes the pain of my life overcomes the promise that you have given to me in your Son. Afraid of disappointment, I choose to believe the worst rather than dare to hope for the best. For me, false hope is more painful than no hope. Without solid evidence given in advance, I would rather cling to the pain of my present circumstances than to risk reaching into the darkness of uncertainty for hope.

During this day, send your Holy Spirit to give me a faith that believes without having to see. Though I doubt, remind me that the Savior doesn't rebuke or upbraid me; rather he walks through my locked doors, enters my presence, speaks "peace", and shows me his scars. When I demand proof or give conditions, please be patient with me. Send the scarred Savior to meet me at my point of need. Before I reach out to him, may he grab my heart and cause it to beat fast. It's in the nail pierced Savior's name that I pray.

Amen

[1]John 20:19-20 [2]John 20:25 [3]John 11:16 [4]John 14:5-6 [5]John 20:27
[6]John 20:28-29

Day 39:

He Knows My Need For Restoration

Scripture Reading: John 21:1-25

Meditation

Simon Peter, more than any of the other disciples, is praying for a second chance.

Peter's the one the Master called "Rock" and yet he was the one who crumbled so easily in the High Priest's courtyard. When a servant girl asked him about his relationship with Jesus, he cracked. Three times he denied knowing his Master. The Rock, now in pieces, longs to have the Savior put his life back together.

As Simon sits between hope and despair, he's not looking for redemption; he knows that Jesus took his sin with him to the cross. He's not even looking for proof of the resurrection; there's been plenty of evidence for that: empty tomb; eyewitness accounts; and even physical appearances by the Messiah marked and certified by the scars. What he's looking for is restoration, a return call to the ministry of his Master. He's wondering if there is any way that he will be able to play some type of role in the Messiah's divine drama.

After his denial, he's no longer expecting to be cast in any principal part. He would be elated with a supporting role. For Peter, any part will do: bit, behind the scenes, chorus. He just wants to be involved in the ongoing story line of the kingdom of God. But only Jesus can give him that. And until Simon knows how the play will be cast, he does what he knows best. He goes back home to the Sea of Galilee and casts his nets.

Simon Peter announced, "I'm going fishing."

The rest of them replied, "We're going with you." They went out and got in the boat. They caught nothing that night. When the sun came up, Jesus was standing on the beach, but they didn't recognize him. [1]

After three years with Jesus, Simon Peter finds himself back where he started—fishing. As he throws and draws his nets, Simon doesn't know if he's still a fisher of men or whether he's denied himself right back into being a fisherman. In truth, he hasn't done very well at either. His spirit is as empty as his nets.

But, just as he promised, Jesus meets Simon Peter at the place where it all began. As Peter and the other disciples are fishing in the early morning hours, Jesus stands on the shore and yells out to them.

"Good morning! Did you catch anything for breakfast?"

They answered, "No."

He said, "Throw the net off the right side of the boat and see what happens."

They did what he said. All of a sudden there were so many fish in it, they weren't strong enough to pull it in. [2]

All of a sudden, so many fish. This is exactly how it all started three years ago. After that first miraculous boatload of fish, Jesus invited them to become fishers of men. Without hesitation, they all left their nets and followed him.

Just like the very first catch of fish, this miracle nets a response. Simon Peter, always the first disciple to jump in, dives into the water and swims the hundred yards toward Jesus. When he reaches the shore, he finds Jesus cooking breakfast on a wood fire. Jesus invites the disciples to eat but the smell of the fire evokes a burning memory for Peter. The smoke of the courtyard denial still clings to him and he still clings to it.

After breakfast, Jesus pulls Peter aside and asks him,

"Simon, son of John, do you love me more than these?" [3]

Under the sharp point of the question is the barb of comparison—*"more than these."* The hook catches the meaty part of Peter's pride and he remembers his presumptuous words. Before the rooster crowed in the courtyard, he had boasted about his fidelity, pointing his braggadocios finger at the others while singling himself out.

"Even if everyone else falls to pieces on account of you, I won't."

"Don't be so sure," Jesus said. "This very night, before the rooster crows up the dawn, you will deny me three times."

Peter protested, "Even if I had to die with you, I would never deny you." [4]

As they continue to talk, Jesus asks Peter two more times about the depth of his love. Unlike the denial in the courtyard, Peter crows three times from the depths of his heart.

"Yes, Master, you know I love you." [5]

With each response, Jesus gives restoration. He makes Peter an under shepherd. He tells him to feed the lambs. But just as the sheep are to follow the shepherd, so also the under shepherd is to follow the Good Shepherd. Jesus warns Peter of what is to come.

> *"I'm telling you the very truth now: When you were young you dressed yourself and went wherever you wished, but when you get old you'll have to stretch out your hands while someone else dresses you and takes you where you don't want to go."*
>
> *He said this to hint at the kind of death by which Peter would glorify God. And then he commanded, "Follow me."* [6]

Simon's been restored. Once again he's to leave his nets but this time he'll take up the Shepherd's staff. Where Jesus leads, Simon is asked to follow. And though the way will lead through the valley of the shadow of death, Jesus assures Peter that the Father will be glorified and that one day he will bring him to dwell in the house of the Lord, restored forever.

Reflection

In what ways are you longing for restoration in your relationship with Christ?

When Jesus says, *"You—Follow me!"* what does that mean? Where is he asking you to go?

During the forty days after Jesus' resurrection, Peter wasn't sure if he was still a fisher of men or a fisherman. Have you ever been confused about your spiritual calling?

How has Christ restored you?

Prayer

Father,

I need more than a second chance; I need restoration. Like Simon Peter, I'm trying to figure out my role in the kingdom. I feel like that there are so many things that I have done that would disqualify me from being a follower of Christ. If I haven't denied your Son with my words, I've betrayed him with my heart. Like Peter, the Rock, my faith and public witness have crumbled so many times. I'm in pieces and I find myself right back where I started, waiting for your Son to speak words of restoration.

During this day, restore me. Show me your Son in an intimate way. Help me see all the ways that he is meeting me anew, just like in the beginning. Remind me of those moments marked forever in my spirit: the call to follow; a life vocation filled with his presence; my steps of faith taken behind his; his provision along the way; all of the promises. When I'm confused about my spiritual calling, assure me that the hand of Christ is outstretched, that his voice is clear, and that he bids me to follow him. Where he leads, may I go. It's in his name that I pray.

Amen

[1]John 21:3-4 [2]John 21:5-6 [3]John 21:15 [4]Matthew 26:33-35 [5]John 21:15 [6]John 21:18-19

He Knows My Co-Mission

Scripture Reading: Matthew 28:16-20

Meditation

What Jesus starts, he always intends to finish.

His three-year public ministry began with his baptism. After forty days of resisting the worldly lures of the Tempter in the wilderness, he began to proclaim good news in the region of Galilee—that, in him, the kingdom of God had arrived.

"Time's up! God's kingdom is here. Change your life and believe the Message." [1]

All throughout Jesus' ministry, this Messianic Message trumpeted the way. His kingdom forcefully advanced, taking devils captive and setting the devil's captives free. The Message was simple and yet it was profound: grace filled with power.

"Jesus of Nazareth is the God-Man, the Messiah promised of old. According to the Scriptures, he will suffer, die, and rise on the third day for the forgiveness of sins. Through him total and eternal life change is available to all."

As Jesus moved throughout Galilee and Judea, the seed of the Messianic kingdom began to take root. By the time the root of Jesse had reached the city of Jerusalem, his kingdom had grown into a tree of life—many branches, much fruit. While in Jerusalem, the tree showed its strength. The debt of sin was nailed to its trunk, death climbed its limbs and ravaged its fruit, and though struck by the devil's ax, the tree budded new life on the third day.

Now it's time for kingdom roots to spread beyond Jerusalem, Judea, and Galilee. It's just not about the natural branches of Israel anymore; there are many foreign limbs that are ready and waiting to be grafted onto the tree. The good news is that even spiritual deadwood has a place on this tree of life. Salvation's fruit hangs low and there's enough for all nations to reap.

In the cross and the empty tomb, the Messianic mission has been accomplished. A commission comes next. The King's Message needs messengers: sent ones authorized and empowered to deliver grace to the grace-less of the earth. The seed of the Message needs to be scattered day after day: every way, everywhere, right up to the end of the age. What the King began needs to continue.

Knowing that his time with his disciples is growing short and that the arm of his gospel message needs to be long extended, Jesus appears to his disciples on a mountain in Galilee. With the authority that he received from his Father, he commissions them.

> *"Go out and train everyone you meet, far and near, in this way of life, marking them by baptism in the three-fold name: Father, Son, and Holy Spirit. Then instruct them in the practice of all I have commanded you. I'll be with you as you do this, day after day after day, right up to the end of the age."* [2]

It's more than a mission; it's a co-mission. He will go with them.

Immanuel—the God with us—will remain true to his nature. Jesus will always be with his disciples. His promise is his presence, no longer visible but always there, among, in and through them. What took place at the incarnation will continue. The Son of God will still be living in their neighborhood. He's not packing up or moving out. He won't leave them orphaned. They're going to do this mission together.

Through them, day after day, far and near, right up to the end of the age, Jesus will finish what he started. He'll speak his words through their mouths. He'll feed, clothe, and tend the hurting through their hands. Their legs will carry him to places where his sandals never walked. He'll give them the keys to the kingdom of heaven and, as they proclaim the Message, they'll see the prisoners set free and the doors of death and Hades bolt shut.

Shortly after the commission on the mountain in Galilee, Jesus gathers with his disciples for the last time. His final words are about the kingdom of God. He reminds them that life in the kingdom isn't about absolute power but amazing grace: sacrifice for sin; servant not lord; denial of self; carrying the cross; a posture of humility over positions of glory. As he finishes, he tells his disciples to go and wait in Jerusalem. The gift that he and his Father had promised—the Holy Spirit—was about to come. The Spirit would bring power to propel them to the ends of the earth.

As soon as his last words were spoken, he was taken up into the air and disappeared into a cloud. As the disciples stood gazing into the sky, two men dressed in white appeared and asked,

> *"You Galileans!—why do you just stand here looking up at an empty sky? This very Jesus who was taken up from among you to heaven will come as certainly—and mysteriously—as he left."* [3]

With one eye to the sky and another to the ends of the earth, the disciples begin. It's more than a mission; it's a co-mission. They don't walk or work alone. But while their Master is at work through them, he's also working in them. He's living and active, finishing what he started in them, until the day he reappears.

"There has never been the slightest doubt in my mind that the God who started this great work in you would keep at it and bring it to a flourishing finish on the very day Christ Jesus appears." [4]

Reflection

What does is mean to be commissioned by Christ?

How is the Great Commission your commission? How does the living and active Christ empower you to carry that mission out?

How does the certainty of Christ's reappearance change the way you lead your life?

Why is it so comforting to know that what Christ started he will also finish?

Prayer

Father,

Like the disciples, I need more than a mission; I need a co-mission. I've had enough of my own well-laid plans and carefully thought out mission statements. I have found that such pursuits promise much but deliver very little. They are void of any lasting meaning. What I long for is an eternal purpose filled with the promise of your Son's presence and fueled by your Spirit's power.

During this day, assure me that, what your Son began in me, he will bring to completion. May he take all of my false starts and abandoned endings and work in them a new beginning. Remind me that, though there is formative work to be done in my life, one day the Savior will bring me to a flourishing finish when he reappears. Thank you for grafting me—spiritual deadwood—into the tree of life. Please use me to bear much fruit for your kingdom. In your Son's name I pray.

Amen.

[1]Mark 1:15 [2]Matthew 28:18-20 [3]Acts 1:11 [4]Philippians 1:6

The Shelter of Eternal Dwelling

"I'm back home in the house of GOD for the rest of my life."

Psalm 23:6b

Turning the bend and heading toward home is the joy that can only come with the journey's end. Home for the sheep is wherever the Shepherd might be. If the Shepherd isn't present then the home just becomes a house, a dwelling where heads may rest but hearts don't stay.

The good news is that, one day, the Shepherd will lead his flock home to forever pastures. Until then, he keeps shepherding.

As you finish these forty days with Christ, reflect on the following ...

Reflection

What does it mean to be *"home in the house of God"?*

Where does your heart feel at home?

One day the Shepherd will lead his flock home to *"forever pastures."* What will that be like?

Epilogue

While I wrote this book, the Good Shepherd took me to places I would have never gone on my own—painful depths as well as exhilarating heights. Maybe the same happened to you as you read it.

For me, each encounter during the forty days was a death and resurrection experience. Daily, the Old Man in me was crucified and buried with Christ so that the New Man might walk out of the tomb, hand in hand with the resurrected Savior. The apostle Paul described it best,

> *Could it be any clearer? Our old way of life was nailed to the Cross with Christ, a decisive end to that sin-miserable life—no longer at sin's every beck and call! What we believe is this: If we get included in Christ's sin-conquering death, we also get included in his life-saving resurrection.* [1]

In the writing, Christ found me where I was; accepted me as I was; but he never left me that way. Each day, as I searched for just the right word, the Word made flesh encountered me. He included me in his *"sin-conquering death"* so that I might also be included in his *"life-saving resurrection."* In the encounter, something about me always changed—more of Christ and less of myself.

As I look back over the past year, I have found that Christ has woven four strands of grace through my life. I pray that, somehow, they have interlaced their way underneath the words and between the lines of this book. Each strand is full of grace and truth. Each is centered on Christ and gives faith something firm to hold onto. Each is tried and true—there isn't any situation where one of these four can't be applied.

If there are only a few words that you take with you from this book, let it be these four final thoughts about Christ.

Christ is for you. In terror of conscience and torment of soul, he's the one who stands high and lifted up and takes the punishment for your sin. He also stands you up when you fall.

Christ lives in you. He's the one who changes you. He does it from the inside out, living his life in your life. Through faith, you're connected to Christ. His death is your death. His life is your life. Daily the sinner goes into the grave and the saint comes out.

Christ works through you. He's living and active in your life. He's doing things through you that you could never dream or imagine. All good works in your life are his works.

Christ is with you. He may be hidden but he said he would always be present. One day he will reappear. You'll see him face to face. Until then, he promised that he would be by your side. He is and always will be Emmanuel—God with us.

He knows your name. More than that, he knows you.

paul
January 13, 2004

[1]Romans 6:6-8